MW00588615

"There are no words to adequately describe how much this consecration means to me. Let Fr. Boniface guide you on a healing journey from the fruitlessness of self-reliance to the fruitful surrender to a loving Mother, who cares for all we need in the paradise of her womb. This is the most powerful consecration to Jesus through Mary that I have ever done and will continue to revisit over and over. It is a sweet and life-changing journey. Thank you, Fr. Boniface!"

—Sr. Thérèse Marie Iglesias, T.O.R.
Franciscan Sisters, T.O.R of Penance
of the Sorrowful Mother

"One of the best things you can do in the spiritual life is consecrate yourself to the Virgin Mary. Nobody knows Jesus better than Mary and, as our spiritual mother, her greatest desire is to bring us closer to Jesus. In *The Fruit of Her Womb*, Fr. Boniface offers us a wonderful program of consecration that employs the wisdom of Sacred Scripture, popes, and saints. I highly recommend this book and encourage everyone to do the consecration!"

—Fr. Donald Calloway, M.I.C.
Author, *Consecration to St. Joseph:*
The Wonders of Our Spiritual Father

"With his experience and heart bringing us into *The Fruit of Her Womb*, Fr. Boniface Hicks, as a skilled cardiac-soul surgeon, accompanies us into the meaning of the refuge and life of the Immaculate and Sacred Hearts. Allow the Holy Spirit, as we slowly listen to this wisdom, to lead us into this light-filled, womb-warmed darkness so we can once again leap—as St. John the Baptist joyfully did—and live our genuine self. When you pick this up, you are the midwife or OB caring for two patients; listening and living the divine cardiac rhythm of *The Fruit of Her Womb*. This is *the* "womb with a view" so desperately needed today."

—**John T. Bruchalski, MD, FACOG**
Founder, Tepeyac OBGYN
President, Divine Mercy Care
Author, *Two Patients: My Conversion*
from *Abortion to Life-Affirming Medicine*

"Fr. Boniface brings a new freshness to Louis de Montfort's time-honored consecration. Rather than holy slavery, Fr. Boniface presents the thirty-three days of preparation through the prism of a loving, filial relationship with Mary, entrusting ourselves to her womb, where she nurtures and forms us into her Son, Jesus. Complete with his own insightful reflections, and a selection of inspired prayers and excerpts from the writings of St. John Paul II, Pope Benedict XVI, Pope Francis, Mother Teresa, and other giants of the Catholic faith, Fr. Boniface breathes new life into the daily exercises of the consecration. This book is truly a needed and accessible Marian consecration for our times."

—**Alicia Goodwin**
Director, Marian Servants of Divine Providence®

"*The Fruit of Her Womb* is a powerful and poignant consecration that will leave you with the deep desire to continually allow our Mother Mary to embrace and receive everything in your life. Appealing to both intellect and emotion through thoughtful and unique reflections, Fr. Boniface invites you to lay your heart bare and be received by the Mother who profoundly loves and tenderly cares for you."

—**Sr. Miriam James Heidland, S.O.L.T.**
Speaker and author

The Fruit of
Her Womb

FR. BONIFACE HICKS, O.S.B.

THE FRUIT OF HER WOMB

33-Day Preparation for Total Consecration to Jesus

❖

Following the Itinerary of St. Louis-Marie Grignion de Montfort with Selections of Writings from the Popes and Saints

SOPHIA INSTITUTE PRESS
MANCHESTER, NH

Imprimi potest:
The Right Reverend Martin R. Bartel, O.S.B.
Archabbot of Saint Vincent Archabbey

Nihil obstat:
The Reverend Monsignor Raymond E. Riffle, VG, MSW, MPA
Censor Librorum

Imprimatur:
The Most Reverend Larry J. Kulick, JCL
Bishop of Greensburg, April 17, 2023

The *nihil obstat, imprimatur,* and *imprimi potest* are official declarations that a book or pamphlet is free of doctrinal or moral error. No implication is contained therein that those who have granted the nihil obstat, imprimatur or imprimi potest agree with the contents, opinions or statements expressed.

Sophia Institute Press
Box 5284, Manchester, NH 03108
1-800-888-9344
www.SophiaInstitute.com

Sophia Institute Press is a registered trademark of Sophia Institute.

paperback ISBN 978-1-64413-840-3
ebook ISBN 978-1-64413-841-0

Library of Congress Control Number: 2023936718

First printing

CONTENTS

Introduction 3

Beginning the Consecration:
Emptying Ourselves of the Spirit of the World

Introduction 11

1. Dependence on God 13
2. Original Sin Poisons Our Thinking 17
3. Save Us from the Prideful Presumption
   of Self-Sufficiency. 21
4. God Hears Our Cry. 25
5. God Reveals Himself to the Childlike. 29
6. The Sign of a Child 33
7. Victory through Love and Patience,
   Not through Power 37
8. Light Dispels Darkness 41
9. Hope in Suffering 45
10. True Love. 49
11. A Christian Interpretation of Reality 53
12. The Great Hope: Love Redeems Us 59

Week of Knowledge of Self

Introduction 65

13. Sharing Christ's Sonship. 67
14. Remaining Little 71

15. Not Judging 75

16. Beloved Sinners: A Dignified Embarrassment 81

17. Pastoral Acedia 87

18. Christian "Diseases" 91

19. Called to Holiness 95

Week of Knowledge of Mary

Introduction 101

20. The Rosary Helps Consecrate Us to Mary 103

21. Mary, Abandoned to God, Becomes Our Mother 107

22. The Weak Are Formed into Christ 111

23. The Holy Name of Mary 115

24. Mary and the Church 119

25. Mary, Our Fiercely Compassionate Mother 123

26. Mary, Our Refuge 127

Week of Knowledge of Jesus Christ

Introduction 133

27. Jesus Is Little, Near, and Real 137

28. Christ Became Poor 141

29. The Humility of Jesus in the Eucharist 147

30. Mary, the Eucharist, and the Incarnation 153

31. God Seeks Man in the Womb of Mary 157

32. Christ Brings Us Life and Light in Baptism 161

33. Jesus Dies, the Word Is Silenced 167

Total Consecration to Jesus through Mary

34. Making Our Total Consecration
    to Jesus through Mary 173

    Act of Total Consecration to Jesus through Mary 177

Appendices

A. St. Louis de Montfort's Consecration 183
B. Prayers 187

   Image Credits 207
   About the Author 211

The Fruit of
Her Womb

Introduction

❖

S t. Louis-Marie Grignion de Montfort set forth a revolution of Christian spirituality when he first taught about Marian consecration and presented his thirty-three-day plan to prepare souls for this big step in their relationship with Jesus.

What is this consecration? St. Louis de Montfort described it as being a form of "slavery" to Mary. This slavery means that we do nothing without her. We choose not to have a will apart from Mary's. St. Louis de Montfort invited us to wear a chain to signify our close bond with her, and he elaborated the consequence of that bond: we share everything with Mary, including our prayers, our intentions, our actions, and our merits. Fundamentally, he said that we choose to become totally dependent on Mary: we receive everything through her and share everything with her.

At first this idea may sound radical, and it may even sound a little scary or seem like a lot of work. As we come to understand the way the spirit of the world has infected our thinking, however, and as we get in touch with our own woundedness, we gradually discover that this consecration is a merciful gift from Heaven and a sweet path of salvation. In fact, it is better than we could have ever hoped for! What this consecration teaches us is that we have a sweet, loving, perfect Mother who actually wants to live in this intense relationship with us. And so, if we accept Mary's invitation to this relationship, we will find all the healing and happiness we have always longed for.

In order to understand our need and desire for a deep relationship with Mary, we have to take a step back and reflect on how we got to where we are.

The principal consequences of Original Sin are a fearful grasping after independence and a repeated search for a security that is in our own control. In the beginning, however, God made us for relationship: first of all with Himself—"then the Lord God formed man of dust from the ground, and breathed into his nostrils the breath of life; and man became a living being" (Gen. 2:7)—and then also with each other—"It is not good that the man should be alone; I will make him a helper fit for him" (Gen. 2:18). These relationships were deeply ruptured by the Fall, when man and woman sought to become gods without God (Gen. 3:1-7). All efforts to achieve immortality through medicine, science, or magic are a consequence of this first sin. Original Sin is behind all our efforts to earn love through our accomplishments or to control our lives through our own power. It is the source of all our unhappiness, emptiness, and fear. It is fundamentally a denial of our being—we did not create ourselves, and we do not have sole power over our destiny. We simply cannot exist without God; trying to do so is a contradiction that splits us in two.

The problem is that living in relationship requires trust, and our trust has been broken over and over, starting with our first infant cry that went unanswered. Our psyches are blistered with broken trust. To whom can we turn for healing?

Fortunately, God does not leave us alone in the wilderness of isolation, nor does He tell us to "get over it" or simply move on, ignoring our hurts. Further, He does not expect us to find our way home on our own, which would only exacerbate the problem. Rather, God reveals Himself as a Father who is trustworthy, and He has sent us His Son to adopt us into His family and to bring us home to our Father in Heaven. This is the adventure of salvation.

In this adventure, we must relearn trust and dependence. And so, because it is not good for the man to be alone (i.e., without human relationships), Jesus also adopts us into His Holy Family, which means that in addition to the imperfect human parents who gave us life, God has also sent us the Blessed Virgin Mary as our perfect human Mother and St. Joseph, Mary's most chaste spouse, as our human father.

Mary fills in any gaps left in us by our birth-mother's limitations. She is the first of the redeemed. She is without sin from the moment of her conception. She will never fail us, forget us, abandon us, or forsake us. She will never break our trust. In this way, she teaches us to trust again and helps to heal our wounds.

St. Joseph is the human father God made for Jesus. He perfectly formed the humanity of Jesus as He matured, that is, as He "increased in wisdom and in stature, and in favor with God and man" (Luke 2:52). For that reason, St. Joseph is also the best human father for us. He builds on all the good things our dads have done, and he fills out all the holes they left when their limitations prevented them from being the fathers we needed them to be.

Now we are in a better position to understand Marian consecration. Most fundamentally, it is a choice to be a child like Jesus. In other words, we are choosing to be a child of Mary and Joseph. But a child can still be willful and wander away, so our dependence must be more radical: we are invited to be the *infant* of Mary and Joseph. Think of Jesus' birth in Bethlehem. Jesus did not provide for Himself, but rather He let Mary and Joseph feed Him and hold Him and even change His diapers. Think of the Flight into Egypt and how helpless Jesus was. He did not protect Himself but rather let Himself be carried to safety by Mary and Joseph, who saved Him from Herod's wrath.

St. Louis de Montfort invited us to go even one step further. He wrote:

> Mary received from God a unique dominion over souls enabling her to nourish them and make them more and more godlike. St. Augustine went so far as to say that even in this world all the elect are enclosed in the womb of Mary, and that their real birthday is when this good mother brings them forth to eternal life. Consequently, just as an infant draws all its nourishment from its mother, who gives according to its needs, so the elect draw their spiritual nourishment and all their strength from Mary.[1]

We therefore must be even more helpless than an infant: we must let ourselves be held in the most perfect embrace of the most loving Mother as a baby in the womb. This is the radical quality of our trust, our abandonment to the one who always perfectly lives in accord with the will of God. Mary is the perfect Mother who will only nourish the child in her womb with the best of foods and who turns every squirming movement of that tiny child into a beautiful expression of love for God.

Of course, there is no greater "slavery" than being in the womb. A baby in the womb is totally helpless and totally dependent on the mother. A baby in the womb has no will other than the will of the mother. And yet the concept of being in our

---

[1] St. Louis de Montfort, *The Secret of Mary*, no. 14, http://www. montfortian.info/writings/the-secret-of-mary.html.

mother's womb holds none of the negative connotations that "slavery" has. While we recognize that slavery is in the Bible and it is not problematic in a theological sense, we also understand that, especially in light of our American history with slavery, the term "slavery" may distract our readers from the essence of the consecration. Marian consecration is first and foremost about love and trust, and it carries none of the harmful or ambiguous connotations of the term "slavery." We have therefore reframed the Total Consecration to Mary, without losing anything, to be no longer described as slavery but as the perfect embrace and safe protection a mother provides for an infant in her womb.

In the following pages, we will embark on a thirty-three-day preparation for Marian consecration after the model given to us by St. Louis de Montfort. We will spend the first twelve days emptying ourselves of the spirit of the world. Then we will spend a week focused on self-knowledge, then a week focused on knowledge of Mary, and finally a week focused on knowledge of Jesus. After thirty-three days of preparation, we will be ready to make a consecration on the thirty-fourth day.

We recommend spending at least ten minutes every day on this preparation for consecration: this includes time to read the teaching provided, to reflect on it, and to recite some prayers to ask for God's grace in this process. The suggested prayers for each day are arranged alphabetically by title at the end of this book.

Whether you are making this journey for the first time or are renewing your consecration, we hope that you will open your heart to the possibility of profound conversion.

We conclude with an encouraging word from St. Louis de Montfort that reminds us that the paradise of Mary's womb is a place of wonders especially fashioned according to each one's weaknesses, a place in which we are only expected to be a little child. Our thirty-three days of preparation open up to us the secret of Mary, in whom we draw closest to our loving God. There is a place for everyone in the bosom of our loving Mother:

> Happy, indeed sublimely happy, is the person to whom the Holy Spirit reveals the secret of Mary, thus imparting to him true knowledge of her. Happy the person to whom the Holy Spirit opens this enclosed garden for him to enter, and to whom the Holy Spirit gives access to this sealed fountain where he can draw water and drink deep draughts of the living waters of grace. That person will find only grace and no creature in the most lovable Virgin Mary. But he will find that the infinitely holy and exalted God is at the same time infinitely solicitous for him and understands his weaknesses. Since God is everywhere, He can be found everywhere, even in Hell. But there is no place where God can be more present to His creature and more sympathetic to human weakness than in Mary. It was indeed for this very purpose that He came down from Heaven. Everywhere else He is the Bread of the strong and the Bread of angels, but living in Mary He is the Bread of children.[2]

Beginning the Consecration: Emptying Ourselves of the Spirit of the World

❖

Introduction

One of the consequences of Original Sin is that we have been tainted by a spirit of independence, self-sufficiency, and grasping at control. We need to see and understand this spirit so that we might recognize how Original Sin has invaded our thinking. Over the next few days, therefore, we will seek the wisdom God gave us through one of the greatest teachers of our time, Pope Benedict XVI, to help us understand our own weakness.

We also need the grace to turn away from the spirit of the world. We must pray earnestly for this grace and perhaps seek various forms of self-sacrifice, targeting for removal those areas that further the spirit of the world. Intellectually, we would do well to fast from content on media that propagates the lies; TV, Netflix, secular news sources, Facebook, and other forms of social media reinforce the thinking that is poisoned by Original Sin. We can also cut back on those things and activities we turn to as a substitute for prayer, such as comfort food, alcohol, shopping, romance novels, over-exercising, excessive work, or others.

Some self-knowledge is important here, and also consultation with a close spiritual friend or spiritual director.

With prayer and self-sacrifice, then, let us begin our spiritual journey.

Dependence on God

Reading 1 *Genesis 3:1–7*

Now the serpent was more subtle than any other wild creature that the Lord God had made. He said to the woman, "Did God say, 'You shall not eat of any tree of the garden'?" And the woman said to the serpent, "We may eat of the fruit of the trees of the garden; but God said, 'You shall not eat of the fruit of the tree which is in the midst of the garden, neither shall you touch it, lest you die.'" But the serpent said to the woman, "You will not die. For God knows that when you eat of it your eyes will be opened, and you will be like God, knowing good and evil." So when the woman saw that the tree was good for food, and that it was a delight to the eyes, and that the tree was to be desired to make one wise, she took of its fruit and ate; and she also gave some to her husband, and he ate. Then the eyes of both were opened, and they knew that they were naked; and they sewed fig leaves together and made themselves aprons.

Reading 2 *Pope Benedict XVI's homily on the Solemnity of the Immaculate Conception, December 8, 2005*

If we set ourselves with the believing and praying Church to listen to this text, then we can begin to understand what Original

Sin, inherited sin, is and also what the protection against this inherited sin is, what redemption is.

What picture does this passage show us? The human being does not trust God. Tempted by the serpent, he harbors the suspicion that in the end, God takes something away from his life, that God is a rival who curtails our freedom and that we will be fully human only when we have cast Him aside; in brief, that only in this way can we fully achieve our freedom.

The human being lives in the suspicion that God's love creates a dependence and that he must rid himself of this dependency if he is to be fully himself. Man does not want to receive his existence and the fullness of his life from God.

He himself wants to obtain from the tree of knowledge the power to shape the world, to make himself a god, raising himself to God's level, and to overcome death and darkness with his own efforts. He does not want to rely on love that to him seems untrustworthy; he relies solely on his own knowledge since it confers power upon him. Rather than on love, he sets his sights on power, with which he desires to take his own life autonomously in hand. And in doing so, he trusts in deceit rather than in truth and thereby sinks with his life into emptiness, into death.

Love is not dependence but a gift that makes us live. The freedom of a human being is the freedom of a limited being, and therefore is itself limited. We can possess it only as a shared freedom, in the communion of freedom: only if we live in the right way, with one another and for one another, can freedom develop.

We live in the right way if we live in accordance with the truth of our being, and that is, in accordance with God's will. For God's will is not a law for the human being imposed from the outside and that constrains him, but the intrinsic measure of his nature, a measure that is engraved within him and makes him the image of God, hence, a free creature.

If we live in opposition to love and against the truth—in opposition to God—then we destroy one another and destroy the world. Then we do not find life but act in the interests of death. All this is recounted with immortal images in the history of the original fall of man and the expulsion of man from the earthly Paradise.

Reflection

Where can you see this thinking in your own life? In what ways are you suspicious of love? Unwilling to ask for help? Rebellious against God's law? Do you fear that God wants to take something away from you? Are you willing to rely on Him for everything? In what ways do you seek a security in your own control?

A baby in the womb is so radically dependent on the mother but also so perfectly provided for. God has given us in Mary and in the Church a mother who wants to provide everything for us as she forms us in her womb.

Prayers

Veni Sancte Spiritus
Ave Maris Stella or Sub Tuum Praesidium
Litany of Penance or Radiating Christ

Original Sin Poisons Our Thinking

Reading 1
Philippians 2:1–8

So if there is any encouragement in Christ, any incentive of love, any participation in the Spirit, any affection and sympathy, complete my joy by being of the same mind, having the same love, being in full accord and of one mind. Do nothing from selfishness or conceit, but in humility count others better than yourselves. Let each of you look not only to his own interests, but also to the interests of others. Have this mind among yourselves, which was in Christ Jesus, who, though he was in the form of God, did not count equality with God a thing to be grasped, but emptied himself, taking the form of a servant, being born in the likeness of men. And being found in human form he humbled himself and became obedient unto death, even death on a cross.

Reading 2
Pope Benedict XVI's homily on the
Solemnity of the Immaculate Conception,
December 8, 2005

Dear brothers and sisters, if we sincerely reflect about ourselves and our history, we have to say that with this narrative [in Gen. 3:1–7] is described not only the history of the beginning but the

history of all times, and that we all carry within us a drop of the poison of that way of thinking, illustrated by the images in the book of Genesis.

We call this drop of poison "Original Sin." Precisely on the Feast of the Immaculate Conception, we have a lurking suspicion that a person who does not sin must really be basically boring and that something is missing from his life: the dramatic dimension of being autonomous; that the freedom to say no, to descend into the shadows of sin and to want to do things on one's own is part of being truly human; that only then can we make the most of all the vastness and depth of our being men and women, of being truly ourselves; that we should put this freedom to the test, even in opposition to God, in order to become, in reality, fully ourselves.

In a word, we think that evil is basically good, we think that we need it, at least a little, in order to experience the fullness of being. We think that Mephistopheles—the tempter—is right when he says he is the power "that always wants evil and always does good" (J. W. von Goethe, *Faust* I, 3). We think that a little bargaining with evil, keeping for oneself a little freedom against God, is basically a good thing, perhaps even necessary.

If we look, however, at the world that surrounds us, we can see that this is not so; in other words, that evil is always poisonous, does not uplift human beings but degrades and humiliates them. It does not make them any the greater, purer, or wealthier, but harms and belittles them.

Reflection

Do I ever think that if I am "too good" life will be boring? Do I think that goodness is boring? Do I try to leave a little room for evil in my life, maybe on the weekend or just on Friday night or on vacation or after everyone has gone to bed? Am I only good when my spouse is nearby or when an authority figure is watching me? Do I gloss over my sinfulness and justify it, perhaps even in the confessional, with a phrase such as "Boys will be boys" or

"You gotta have a little fun!"? Can I hear God calling me to a deeper conversion, to shut down these outlets and pursue goodness more wholeheartedly?

No one lived a more exciting life than Jesus and Mary. Think of how exciting it was from the very beginning, when Jesus was conceived in the womb of Mary at the Annunciation, or when Mary carried Him in her womb to her cousin Elizabeth, whose infant, John the Baptist, "leaped in her womb" at the sound of Mary's greeting (Luke 1:41). When we are willing to live in such a constant, dependent relationship with Mary by being in her womb, life will only become more exciting, full, and rich.

Prayers

Veni Sancte Spiritus
Ave Maris Stella or Sub Tuum Praesidium
Litany of Penance or Radiating Christ

Save Us from the Prideful Presumption of Self-Sufficiency

Reading 1 *Luke 5:30–32*

The Pharisees and their scribes murmured against his disciples, saying, "Why do you eat and drink with tax collectors and sinners?" And Jesus answered them, "Those who are well have no need of a physician, but those who are sick; I have not come to call the righteous, but sinners to repentance."

Reading 2 *Pope Benedict XVI's* Urbi et Orbi *Christmas Message, December 25, 2011*

This is how Christ is invoked in an ancient liturgical antiphon: "O Emmanuel, our king and lawgiver, hope and salvation of the peoples: come to save us, O Lord our God." *Veni ad salvandum nos!* Come to save us! This is the cry raised by men and women in every age, who sense that by themselves they cannot prevail over difficulties and dangers. They need to put their hands in a greater and stronger hand, a hand which reaches out to them from on high. Dear brothers and sisters, this hand is Christ, born in

Bethlehem of the Virgin Mary. He is the hand that God extends to humanity, to draw us out of the mire of sin and to set us firmly on rock, the secure rock of His Truth and His Love (cf. Ps. 40:2).

This is the meaning of the Child's name, the name which, by God's will, Mary and Joseph gave Him: He is named Jesus, which means "Savior" (cf. Matt. 1:21; Luke 1:31). He was sent by God the Father to save us above all from the evil deeply rooted in man and in history: the evil of separation from God, the prideful presumption of being self-sufficient, of trying to compete with God and to take His place, to decide what is good and evil, to be the master of life and death (cf. Gen. 3:1–7). This is the great evil, the great sin, from which we human beings cannot save ourselves unless we rely on God's help, unless we cry out to Him: "*Veni ad salvandum nos!* Come to save us!"

Reflection

God does not answer prayers that cause us to need Him less. He is trying to save us from being alone and from needing no one. Generally, when we go to an earthly physician, we hope that our issue will be resolved well enough that we never need to see him again. This is not the approach of the Divine Physician: He seeks to treat us so that we never try to go without Him again, because He Himself is the cure. Let us reflect on the ways we might try to use God in order to need God less.

A baby in the womb is radically dependent on his or her mother, and a preterm baby is never better off being outside of the womb. Even if a baby must be born prematurely, the doctors care for him or her best by creating an environment that is as much like the womb as possible. A baby with a perfect, loving mother cannot find a better place to grow in love and life than in the womb. And so Mary, our perfect Mother, nurtures and protects us until we are ready to be born into eternal life.

Prayers

Veni Sancte Spiritus
Ave Maris Stella or Sub Tuum Praesidium
Litany of Penance or Radiating Christ

God Hears Our Cry

Reading 1 *Romans 7:15–20; 8:12–17*

I do not understand my own actions. For I do not do what I want, but I do the very thing I hate. Now if I do what I do not want, I agree that the law is good. So then it is no longer I that do it, but sin which dwells within me. For I know that nothing good dwells within me, that is, in my flesh. I can will what is right, but I cannot do it. For I do not do the good I want, but the evil I do not want is what I do. Now if I do what I do not want, it is no longer I that do it, but sin which dwells within me....

So then, brethren, we are debtors, not to the flesh, to live according to the flesh—for if you live according to the flesh you will die, but if by the Spirit you put to death the deeds of the body you will live. For all who are led by the Spirit of God are sons of God. For you did not receive the spirit of slavery to fall back into fear, but you have received the spirit of sonship. When we cry, "Abba! Father!" it is the Spirit himself bearing witness with our spirit that we are children of God, and if children, then heirs, heirs of God and fellow heirs with Christ, provided we suffer with him in order that we may also be glorified with him.

Reading 2

Pope Benedict XVI's Urbi et Orbi
Christmas Message, December 25, 2011

This is the great evil, the great sin, from which we human beings cannot save ourselves unless we rely on God's help, unless we cry out to Him: "*Veni ad salvandum nos!* Come to save us!"

The very fact that we cry to Heaven in this way already sets us aright; it makes us true to ourselves: we are in fact those who cried out to God and were saved (cf. Esther [LXX] 10:3ff.). God is the Savior; we are those who are in peril. He is the physician; we are the infirm. To realize this is the first step towards salvation, towards emerging from the maze in which we have been locked by our pride. To lift our eyes to Heaven, to stretch out our hands and call for help is our means of escape, provided that there is Someone who hears us and can come to our assistance.

Jesus Christ is the proof that God has heard our cry. And not only this! God's love for us is so strong that He cannot remain aloof; He comes out of Himself to enter into our midst and to share fully in our human condition (cf. Exod. 3:7-12). The answer to our cry which God gave in Jesus infinitely transcends our expectations, achieving a solidarity which cannot be human alone, but divine. Only the God who is love, and the love which is God, could choose to save us in this way, which is certainly the lengthiest way, yet the way which respects the truth about Him and about us: the way of reconciliation, dialogue, and cooperation.

Reflection

Do I recognize that I cannot save myself? Do I believe that God will always hear my cry? Do I acknowledge that Jesus Himself is the answer to my cry, that He is God who has come close to me, and that He will never abandon me? Do I really believe that He is my Savior?

We are crying for a home, crying to belong, crying for the things we need to grow, crying to make sense of the pain and find support, crying for others. When we cry out, Mary responds to us and brings us into her arms and then into that tighter, safer, more beautiful embrace in her womb. In coming to share our human condition, Jesus made Mary's womb the perfect place for all our needs to be met and also the place that we can always find Him, who is always the Son of Mary.

Prayers

Veni Sancte Spiritus
Ave Maris Stella or Sub Tuum Praesidium
Litany of Penance or Radiating Christ

God Reveals Himself to the Childlike

Reading 1 *Matthew 11:25–27*

At that time Jesus declared, "I thank thee, Father, Lord of heaven and earth, that thou hast hidden these things from the wise and understanding and revealed them to babes; yea, Father, for such was thy gracious will. All things have been delivered to me by my Father; and no one knows the Son except the Father, and no one knows the Father except the Son and anyone to whom the Son chooses to reveal him."

Reading 2 *Pope Benedict XVI's homily for Mass
with the members of the International
Theological Commission, December 1, 2009*

We have heard that our Lord praises the Father because He concealed the great mystery of the Son, the Trinitarian mystery, the Christological mystery, from the wise and the learned, from those who did not recognize Him. Instead He revealed it to children, the *nèpioi*, to those who are not learned, who are not very cultured. It was to them that this great mystery was revealed....

In our time there have also been "little ones" who have understood this mystery. Let us think of St. Bernadette Soubirous; of

St. Thérèse of Lisieux, with her new interpretation of the Bible that is "non-scientific" but goes to the heart of Sacred Scripture; of the saints and blesseds of our time: St. Josephine Bakhita, St. Teresa of Calcutta, St. Damien de Veuster—we could list so many!

But from all this the question arises: "Why should this be so?" Is Christianity the religion of the foolish, of people with no culture or who are uneducated? Is faith extinguished where reason is kindled? How can this be explained? Perhaps we should take another look at history. What Jesus said, what can be noted in all the centuries, is true. Nevertheless, there is a "type" of lowly person who is also learned. Our Lady stood beneath the Cross, the humble handmaid of the Lord and the great woman illumined by God. And John was there too, a fisherman from

the Sea of Galilee. He is the John whom the Church was rightly to call "the theologian," for he was really able to see the mystery of God and proclaim it: eagled-eyed he entered into the inaccessible light of the divine mystery. So it was too that after His Resurrection, the Lord, on the road to Damascus, touches the heart of Saul, one of those learned people who cannot see. He himself, in his First Letter to Timothy, writes that he was "acting ignorantly" at that time, despite his knowledge. But the Risen One touches him: he is blinded. Yet at the same time, he truly gains sight; he begins to see. The great scholar becomes a "little one" and for this very reason perceives the folly of God as wisdom, a wisdom far greater than all human wisdom.

We could continue to interpret the holy story in this way. Just one more observation. These erudite terms, *sofòi* and *sinetòi*, in the First Reading [Isa. 11:1–10] are used in a different way. Here *sofia* and *sinesis* are gifts of the Holy Spirit which descend upon the Messiah, upon Christ. What does this mean? It turns out that there is a dual use of reason and a dual way of being either wise or little....

Then there is the other way of using reason, of being wise—that of the man who recognizes who he is; he recognizes the proper measure and greatness of God, opening himself in humility to the newness of God's action. It is in this way, precisely by accepting his own smallness, making himself little as he really is, that he arrives at the truth. Thus reason too can express all its possibilities; it is not extinguished but rather grows and becomes greater. *Sofia* and *sinesis* in this context do not exclude one from the mystery that is real communion with the Lord, in whom reside wisdom and knowledge and their truth.

Let us now pray that the Lord will give us true humility. May He give us the grace of being little in order to be truly wise; may He illumine us, enable us to see His mystery in the joy of the Holy Spirit.

Reflection

Do I see my own littleness? Do I see the greatness of God? Let us pray for true humility and the grace of littleness.

Mary's womb is the Seat of Wisdom, where we can be both little and wise. It is where we learn the Wisdom of Jesus, who saved us by becoming small and weak. When we place ourselves in Mary's womb and do all of our reasoning from that perspective, we take ourselves less seriously, empty out our intellectual pride, and learn to delight in the wonders of God. We should think of the Baby Jesus in Mary's lap as He reaches out to discover the world from a place of perfect love and safety.

Prayers

Veni Sancte Spiritus
Ave Maris Stella or Sub Tuum Praesidium
Litany of Penance or Radiating Christ

The Sign of a Child

Reading 1 *Luke 2:8–14*

And in that region there were shepherds out in the field, keeping watch over their flock by night. And an angel of the Lord appeared to them, and the glory of the Lord shone around them, and they were filled with fear. And the angel said to them, "Be not afraid; for behold, I bring you good news of a great joy which will come to all the people; for to you is born this day in the city of David a Savior, who is Christ the Lord. And this will be a sign for you: you will find a babe wrapped in swaddling cloths and lying in a manger." And suddenly there was with the angel a multitude of the heavenly host praising God and saying, "Glory to God in the highest, and on earth peace among men with whom he is pleased."

Reading 2 *Pope Benedict XVI's Midnight Mass homily, December 24, 2006*

We have just heard in the Gospel the message given by the angels to the shepherds during that Holy Night, a message which the Church now proclaims to us: "To you is born this day in the city of David a Savior, who is Christ the Lord. And this will be a sign for you: you will find a babe wrapped in swaddling clothes and lying in a manger" (Luke 2:11–12). Nothing miraculous, nothing

extraordinary, nothing magnificent is given to the shepherds as a sign. All they will see is a Child wrapped in swaddling clothes, One who, like all children, needs a mother's care; a Child born in a stable, who therefore lies not in a cradle but in a manger. God's sign is the Baby in need of help and in poverty. Only in their hearts will the shepherds be able to see that this Baby fulfills the promise of the prophet Isaiah, which we heard in the first reading: "For to us a child is born, to us a son is given; and the government will be upon his shoulder" (Isa. 9:5). Exactly the same sign has been given to us. We too are invited by the angel of God, through the message of the Gospel, to set out in our hearts to see the Child lying in the manger.

God's sign is simplicity. God's sign is the Baby. God's sign is that He makes Himself small for us. This is how He reigns. He does not come with power and outward splendor. He comes as a Baby—defenseless and in need of our help. He does not want to overwhelm us with His strength. He takes away our fear of His greatness. He asks for our love: so He makes Himself a Child. He wants nothing from us other than our love, through which we spontaneously learn to enter into His feelings, His thoughts, and His will—we learn to live with Him and to practice with Him that humility of renunciation that belongs to the very essence of love. God made Himself small so that we could understand Him, welcome Him, and love Him.

Reflection

Let us meditate on the little God who comes to us, and let us welcome Him into our arms and our hearts and love Him.

We learn to see Him better as we become more like Him. When we choose to become little and accept our weakness, we draw closer to the Baby Jesus in the womb of Mary. As we love Him, we enter into His feelings, His thoughts, and His will, and we enter into the heart and into the womb of Mary, to whom He first entrusted His life. There, we will find ourselves pressed up against Him like twins in the womb, and we will experience His paradise in a place of perfect love.

Prayers

Veni Sancte Spiritus
Ave Maris Stella or Sub Tuum Praesidium
Litany of Penance or Radiating Christ

Victory through Love and Patience, Not through Power

Reading 1 *Romans 8:18–25*

I consider that the sufferings of this present time are not worth comparing with the glory that is to be revealed to us. For the creation waits with eager longing for the revealing of the sons of God; for the creation was subjected to futility, not of its own will but by the will of him who subjected it in hope; because the creation itself will be set free from its bondage to decay and obtain the glorious liberty of the children of God. We know that the whole creation has been groaning in travail together until now; and not only the creation, but we ourselves, who have the first fruits of the Spirit, groan inwardly as we wait for adoption as sons, the redemption of our bodies. For in this hope we were saved. Now hope that is seen is not hope. For who hopes for what he sees? But if we hope for what we do not see, we wait for it with patience.

Reading 2

Pope Benedict XVI's homily for his inaugural Mass, April 24, 2005

In the Ancient Near East, it was customary for kings to style themselves shepherds of their people. This was an image of their power, a cynical image: to them their subjects were like sheep, which the shepherd could dispose of as he wished. When the Shepherd of all humanity, the living God, Himself became a Lamb, He stood on the side of the lambs, with those who are downtrodden and killed. This is how He reveals Himself to be the true Shepherd: "I am the Good Shepherd ... I lay down my life for the sheep," Jesus says of Himself (John 10:14-15). It is not power but love that redeems us! This is God's sign: He Himself is love. How often we wish that God would show Himself stronger, that He would strike decisively, defeating evil and creating a better world. All ideologies of power justify themselves in exactly this way, they justify the destruction of whatever would stand in the way of progress and the liberation of humanity. We suffer on account of God's patience. And yet, we need His patience. God, who became a Lamb, tells us that the world is saved by the Crucified One, not by those who crucified Him. The world is redeemed by the patience of God. It is destroyed by the impatience of man.

Reflection

Do I wish for the destruction of my enemies? Do I pray that God would show Himself the stronger and strike decisively against those who could hurt me? Do I suffer because of God's patience?

One of the first threats that Jesus faced was from King Herod. Think of the helplessness of Jesus when He was threatened by Herod's power. Jesus was a baby: He had no voice, no understanding, no plan, no defense. God, however, chose not to destroy Herod but to warn Joseph in a dream to take Mary and

the Child and flee to Egypt. God Himself remained hidden and helpless.

Learning the patience of the little Lamb of God is so hard, but it is possible when we trust Mary and Joseph to take care of us as they took care of Jesus. Make an act of trust in God, who is taking care of everything and working out His plan of salvation. Make an act of love to unite your sufferings to the sufferings of Christ.

Prayers

Veni Sancte Spiritus
Ave Maris Stella or Sub Tuum Praesidium
Litany of Penance or Radiating Christ

Light Dispels Darkness

Reading 1 *Genesis 1:1–5*

In the beginning God created the heavens and the earth. The earth was without form and void, and darkness was upon the face of the deep; and the Spirit of God was moving over the face of the waters.

And God said, "Let there be light"; and there was light. And God saw that the light was good; and God separated the light from the darkness. God called the light Day, and the darkness he called Night. And there was evening and there was morning, one day.

Reading 2 *Pope Benedict XVI's homily for
the Easter Vigil, April 7, 2012*

What is the Creation account saying here? Light makes life possible. It makes encounter possible. It makes communication possible. It makes knowledge, access to reality and to truth, possible. And insofar as it makes knowledge possible, it makes freedom and progress possible. Evil hides. Light, then, is also an expression of the good that both is and creates brightness.

It is daylight, which makes it possible for us to act. To say that God created light means that God created the world as a space for knowledge and truth, as a space for encounter and freedom, as a space for good and for love. Matter is fundamentally good, being itself is good. And evil does not come from God-made being, rather, it comes into existence only through denial. It is a "no."

At Easter, on the morning of the first day of the week, God said once again: "Let there be light." The night on the Mount of Olives, the solar eclipse of Jesus' Passion and death, the night of the grave had all passed. Now it is the first day once again — creation is beginning anew. "Let there be light," says God, "and there was light": Jesus rises from the grave. Life is stronger than death. Good is stronger than evil. Love is stronger than hate. Truth is stronger than lies. The darkness of the previous days is driven away the moment Jesus rises from the grave and Himself becomes God's pure light. But this applies not only to Him, not only to the darkness of those days. With the Resurrection of Jesus, light itself is created anew. He draws all of us after Him into the new light of the Resurrection, and He conquers all darkness. He is God's new day, new for all of us.

But how is this to come about? How does all this affect us so that instead of remaining word it becomes a reality that draws us in? Through the sacrament of Baptism and the profession of faith, the Lord has built a bridge across to us, through which the new day reaches us. The Lord says to the newly-baptized: *Fiat lux*—let there be light. God's new day, the day of indestructible life, comes also to us. Christ takes you by the hand. From now on, you are held by Him and walk with Him into the light, into real life. For this reason the early Church called Baptism *photismos*—illumination.

Reflection

St. Louis de Montfort reminded us that Baptism is an entrance into Mary's womb. It is in Mary's womb that we learn a new logic and are enlightened as to the real power, providence, and plan of God. Here we first draw close to Christ, like twins together in the womb, and we are formed with Him by the Holy Spirit to become another Christ.

Have I allowed the logic of God to be fully formed in me? Do I allow a new light from God to rise up in my mind and heart? Do I believe that "Life is stronger than death, good is stronger than evil, love is stronger than hate, truth is stronger than lies"? Will I take Christ's hand again, as I once did in Baptism, and allow myself to be illumined by the light of His love?

Renew your Baptismal vows: make a profession of faith and recite the Creed.

Prayers

Nicene Creed (I believe in one God …)
Veni Sancte Spiritus
Ave Maris Stella or Sub Tuum Praesidium
Litany of Penance or Radiating Christ

Hope in Suffering

Reading 1 *Colossians 1:24–29*

Now I rejoice in my sufferings for your sake, and in my flesh I complete what is lacking in Christ's afflictions for the sake of his body, that is, the Church, of which I became a minister according to the divine office which was given to me for you, to make the word of God fully known, the mystery hidden for ages and generations but now made manifest to his saints. To them God chose to make known how great among the Gentiles are the riches of the glory of this mystery, which is Christ in you, the hope of glory. Him we proclaim, warning every man and teaching every man in all wisdom, that we may present every man mature in Christ. For this I toil, striving with all the energy which he mightily inspires within me.

Reading 2 *Pope Benedict XVI's encyclical letter*
 Spe salvi *(November 30, 2007), no. 39*

To suffer with the other and for others; to suffer for the sake of truth and justice; to suffer out of love and in order to become a person who truly loves—these are fundamental elements of humanity, and to abandon them would destroy man himself. Yet once again the question arises: are we capable of this? Is the other important enough to warrant my becoming, on his

account, a person who suffers? Does truth matter to me enough to make suffering worthwhile? Is the promise of love so great that it justifies the gift of myself? In the history of humanity, it was the Christian faith that had the particular merit of bringing forth within man a new and deeper capacity for these kinds of suffering that are decisive for his humanity. The Christian faith has shown us that truth, justice, and love are not simply ideals but enormously weighty realities. It has shown us that God—Truth and Love in person—desired to suffer for us and with us. Bernard of Clairvaux coined the marvelous expression: *Impassibilis est Deus, sed non incompassibilis*—God cannot suffer, but He can *suffer with*. Man is worth so much to God that He Himself became man in order to *suffer with* man in an utterly real way—in flesh and blood—as is revealed to us in the account of Jesus' Passion. Hence in all human suffering we are joined by One who experiences and carries that suffering with us; hence *con-solatio* is present in all suffering, the consolation of God's compassionate love—and so the star of hope rises. Certainly, in our many different sufferings and trials we always need the lesser and greater hopes too—a kind visit, the healing of internal and external wounds, a favorable resolution of a crisis, and so on. In our lesser trials these kinds of hope may even be sufficient. But in truly great trials, where I must make a definitive decision to place the truth before my own welfare, career, and possessions, I need the certitude of that true, great hope of which we have spoken here. For this too we need witnesses—martyrs—who have given themselves totally, so as to show us the way—day after day. We need them if we are to prefer goodness to comfort, even in the little choices we face each day—knowing that this is how we live life to the full. Let us say it once again: the capacity to suffer for the sake of the truth is the measure of humanity. Yet this capacity to suffer depends on the type and extent of the hope that we bear within us and build upon. The saints were able to make the great journey of human existence in the way that Christ had done before them, because they were brimming with great hope.

Reflection

In our humanity, if we are apart from God, our solitude becomes like a tomb, where there are dead and dying things. But as Christ enters into our solitude, it becomes like a womb, where we are little and loved, and where there is life and growth. Now, every suffering, every threat, every difficulty becomes only a reminder that I am in the womb of Mary, with Jesus. As things become more intense and the pressure increases, it is only because I am growing and drawing closer to birth, that is, the victorious emergence into eternal life.

Do I have the certitude of that great hope that will not fail, Jesus Christ? Do I find enough strength in that hope to suffer for the sake of truth and for the sake of others? Let us reflect on the little hopes as well as the great hope in our lives and then make an act of hope:

O my God, relying on Your almighty power and infinite mercy and promises, I hope to obtain pardon of my sins, the help of Your grace, and life everlasting, through the merits of Jesus Christ, my Lord and Redeemer. Amen.

Prayers

Veni Sancte Spiritus
Ave Maris Stella or Sub Tuum Praesidium
Litany of Penance or Radiating Christ

True Love

Reading 1 *1 John 4:7–12*

Beloved, let us love one another; for love is of God, and he who loves is born of God and knows God. He who does not love does not know God; for God is love. In this the love of God was made manifest among us, that God sent his only Son into the world, so that we might live through him. In this is love, not that we loved God but that he loved us and sent his Son to be the expiation for our sins. Beloved, if God so loved us, we also ought to love one another. No man has ever seen God; if we love one another, God abides in us and his love is perfected in us.

Reading 2 *Pope Benedict XVI's encyclical letter* *Deus caritas est (December 25, 2005), nos. 5–6*

Nowadays Christianity of the past is often criticized as having been opposed to the body; and it is quite true that tendencies of this sort have always existed. Yet the contemporary way of exalting the body is deceptive. *Eros*, reduced to pure "sex," has become a commodity, a mere "thing" to be bought and sold; or rather, man himself becomes a commodity. This is hardly man's great "yes" to the body. On the contrary, he now considers his body and his sexuality as the purely material part of himself, to be used and exploited at will. Nor does he see it as an arena for the exercise of his freedom but as a mere object that he attempts, as he pleases, to make both enjoyable and harmless. Here we are actually dealing with a debasement of the human body: no longer is it integrated into our overall existential freedom; no longer is it a vital expression of our whole being, but it is more or less relegated to the purely biological sphere. The apparent exaltation of the body can quickly turn into a hatred of bodiliness. Christian faith, on the other hand, has always considered man a unity in duality, a reality in which spirit and matter compenetrate and in which each is brought to a new

nobility. True, *eros* tends to rise "in ecstasy" towards the Divine, to lead us beyond ourselves; yet for this very reason it calls for a path of ascent, renunciation, purification, and healing.

Concretely, what does this path of ascent and purification entail? How might love be experienced so that it can fully realize its human and divine promise? Here we can find a first, important indication in the Song of Songs, an Old Testament book well known to the mystics. According to the interpretation generally held today, the poems contained in this book were originally love songs, perhaps intended for a Jewish wedding feast and meant to exalt conjugal love. In this context, it is highly instructive to note that in the course of the book, two different Hebrew words are used to indicate "love." First there is the word *dodim*, a plural form suggesting a love that is still insecure, indeterminate, and searching. This comes to be replaced by the word *ahabà*, which the Greek version of the Old Testament translates with the similar-sounding *agape*, which, as we have seen, becomes the typical expression for the biblical notion of love. By contrast with an indeterminate, "searching" love, this word expresses the experience of a love which involves a real discovery of the other, moving beyond the selfish character that prevailed earlier. Love now becomes concern and care for the other. No longer is it self-seeking, a sinking in the intoxication of happiness; instead it seeks the good of the beloved: it becomes renunciation and it is ready, and even willing, for sacrifice.

Reflection

The Greek word *eros* that Pope Benedict XVI mentions above means "desire." While this "desire" may be cheapened by some extent into lust, it more accurately means a desire for the whole person, or, in a more spiritual sense, God's deep desire for humanity and our desire for God. We see the intensity of God's *eros* in the Incarnation: God so desires to be with us that He overshadows Mary by the power of the Holy Spirit and becomes Incarnate in her womb. He meets us first in weakness, in littleness, in the womb of Mary. His *eros* drives Him to empty Himself in *agape*, self-sacrificing love, and to unite Himself with our most fragile human experiences.

How does this understanding of love and desire correspond to my idea of love? Where do I get my ideas about love? Do I buy into the lie that sex is simply a bodily experience without meaning or spiritual implication? Do I see the goodness of *eros* and also the way that it must be purified by *agape*?

Let us reflect on any distortions in our view of love and then make an act of love to God:

> O my God, I love You above all things, with my whole heart and soul, because You are all good and worthy of all my love. I love my neighbor as myself for the love of You. I forgive all who have injured me, and I ask pardon of all whom I have injured.

Prayers

Veni Sancte Spiritus
Ave Maris Stella or Sub Tuum Praesidium
Litany of Penance or Radiating Christ

A Christian Interpretation of Reality

Reading 1 *Revelation 5:1–5*

And I saw in the right hand of him who was seated on the throne a scroll written within and on the back, sealed with seven seals; and I saw a strong angel proclaiming with a loud voice, "Who is worthy to open the scroll and break its seals?" And no one in heaven or on earth or under the earth was able to open the scroll or to look into it, and I wept much that no one was found worthy to open the scroll or to look into it. Then one of the elders said to me, "Weep not; lo, the Lion of the tribe of Judah, the Root of David, has conquered, so that he can open the scroll and its seven seals."

Reading 2 *Pope Benedict XVI's General Audience, September 12, 2012*

What do these symbols mean? They remind us of the way to take to be able to interpret the events of history and of our own life. By raising our gaze to God's Heaven, in a constant relationship with Christ, opening our hearts and minds to Him in personal and community prayer, we learn to see things in a new light and to perceive their truest meaning. Prayer is, as it were, an open window that enables us to keep our gaze turned to God, not only to remember the destination towards which we are bound but also to let God's will illuminate our earthly pilgrimage and help us live it with intensity and commitment.

How does the Lord guide the Christian community to a deeper interpretation of history? First of all by asking it to consider the present that we are living in realistically. The Lamb then opens the first four seals of the scroll, and the Church sees the world in which it is inserted, a world in which there are various negative elements. There are the wicked deeds of men and women, such as acts of violence that stem from the desire to possess, to dominate each other, even to the point of self-destruction (the second seal); or injustice, because people fail to respect the laws that they have given themselves (the third seal). To these are added the evils that human beings must suffer, such as death, hunger, and pestilence (the fourth seal).

In the face of these all too often dramatic situations, the ecclesial community is asked never to lose hope, to believe firmly that the apparent omnipotence of the Evil One comes up against the real almightiness which is God's. And the first seal which the Lamb breaks open contains this very message. John recounts: "And I saw, and behold, a white horse, and its rider had a bow; and a crown was given to him, and he went out conquering and to conquer" (Rev. 6:2). God's power that cannot only offset evil but can actually overcome it, entered human history. The color white refers to the Resurrection: God made Himself so close that He came down into the darkness of death to illuminate it with the splendor of His divine life; He took the evil of the world upon His own shoulders to purify it with the fire of His love.

How can we develop in this Christian interpretation of reality? The book of Revelation tells us that prayer nourishes this

vision of light and of deep hope in each one of us and in our communities: it invites us not to let ourselves be overcome by evil but to overcome evil with good, to look at the Crucified and Risen Christ who associates us with His victory. The Church lives in history: she does not withdraw into herself but courageously continues on her journey through difficulty and suffering, forcefully asserting that in the end evil does not overcome good, that darkness does not conceal God's splendor. This is an important point for us: as Christians we can never be pessimistic; we know well that on our journey through life we often encounter violence, falsehood, hatred, and persecution, but this does not discourage us. Prayer teaches us above all to see God's signs, His presence, and His action, indeed, to be lights of goodness ourselves, spreading hope and showing that the victory is God's.

Reflection

How do I see reality? Do I try to develop a Christian interpretation of reality through prayer, or do I let the evening news or my favorite pundits form my interpretation of reality? Do I give in to pessimism or cynicism? Do I try to overcome evil with good? Do I believe that God wins the victory and that He makes all things new?

God turned our human logic on its head when He chose to enter this world in hiddenness and weakness: He came not as a powerful king or a mighty warrior but as a tiny Infant in the womb of Mary. He kept this posture throughout His whole life, until He died as a King crowned with thorns and a warrior armed only with a Cross.

By remaining spiritually in the womb of Mary, we can see the fingerprints of God in history and face future trials with hope through the eyes of the true, Infant King.

Prayers

Veni Sancte Spiritus
Ave Maris Stella or Sub Tuum Praesidium
Litany of Penance or Radiating Christ

The Great Hope: Love Redeems Us

Reading 1 *Romans 8:28, 35–39*

We know that in everything God works for good with those who love him, who are called according to his purpose.... Who shall separate us from the love of Christ? Shall tribulation, or distress, or persecution, or famine, or nakedness, or peril, or sword? As it is written, "For thy sake we are being killed all the day long; we are regarded as sheep to be slaughtered." No, in all these things we are more than conquerors through him who loved us. For I am sure that neither death, nor life, nor angels, nor principalities, nor things present, nor things to come, nor powers, nor height, nor depth, nor anything else in all creation, will be able to separate us from the love of God in Christ Jesus our Lord.

Reading 2 *Pope Benedict XVI's encyclical letter* Spe salvi *(November 30, 2007), nos. 25–27*

Francis Bacon and those who followed in the intellectual current of modernity that he inspired were wrong to believe that man would be redeemed through science. Such an expectation asks too much of science; this kind of hope is deceptive. Science

can contribute greatly to making the world and mankind more human. Yet it can also destroy mankind and the world unless it is steered by forces that lie outside it. On the other hand, we must also acknowledge that modern Christianity, faced with the successes of science in progressively structuring the world, has to a large extent restricted its attention to the individual and his salvation. In so doing, it has limited the horizon of its hope and has failed to recognize sufficiently the greatness of its task—even if it has continued to achieve great things in the formation of man and in care for the weak and the suffering.

It is not science that redeems man: man is redeemed by love. This applies even in terms of this present world. When someone has the experience of a great love in his life, this is a moment of "redemption" which gives a new meaning to his life. But soon he will also realize that the love bestowed upon him cannot by itself resolve the question of his life. It is a love that remains fragile. It can be destroyed by death. The human being needs unconditional love. He needs the certainty which makes him say: "neither death, nor life, nor angels, nor principalities, nor things present, nor things to come, nor powers, nor height, nor depth, nor anything else in all creation, will be able to separate us from the love of God in Christ Jesus our Lord" (Rom. 8:38-39). If this absolute love exists, with its absolute certainty, then—only then—is man "redeemed," whatever should happen to him in his particular circumstances. This is what it means to say: Jesus Christ has "redeemed" us. Through Him we have become certain of God, a God who is not a remote "first cause" of the world because His only-begotten Son has become man, and of Him everyone can say: "I live by faith in the Son of God, who loved me and gave himself for me" (Gal. 2:20).

In this sense, it is true that anyone who does not know God, even though he may entertain all kinds of hopes, is ultimately without hope, without the great hope that sustains the whole of life (cf. Eph. 2:12). Man's great, true hope which holds firm in spite of all disappointments can only be God—God who has loved us and who continues to love us "to the end," until all "is accomplished" (cf. John 13:1 and 19:30). Whoever is moved by love begins to perceive what "life" really is.

Reflection

Do I ask too much of science? Do I place too much hope in medicine and technology? Have I experienced a moment of redemption through a great love in my life? Have I also experienced the fragility of this love? Do I believe in an absolute love that is not threatened by death, namely the love of God revealed in Christ Jesus?

I can learn the unconditional love of God revealed in Jesus Christ by being pressed up against Him as His twin in the womb of Mary. As much as I face uncertainties in life, I do not face them alone. As much as I struggle with suffering and groan for redemption, I know that I am only going through preparation for birth and that Christ is with me and goes before me as the firstborn. No baby is stillborn from the womb of Mary.

Prayers

> Veni Sancte Spiritus
> Ave Maris Stella or Sub Tuum Praesidium
> Litany of Penance or Radiating Christ

Week of Knowledge
of Self

❖

Introduction

❖

Now that we have emptied ourselves of the spirit of the world, St. Louis de Montfort asks us to spend a week deepening our self-knowledge before we look more closely at who Mary and Jesus are.

Who are we, then?

By Baptism, we can confidently say that we are beloved children of God. We are baptized into Jesus Christ, and so we share His Sonship with the Father. Moreover, as children of the Heavenly Father in Christ Jesus, we are children of His Mother, Mary, as well.

Baptism has freed us from sin, although we know that we continue to struggle with weaknesses, imperfections, and even sins. As we focus on growing in self-knowledge, we should remember that it is good and healthy for us to understand our own shortcomings and sins so that we can receive the grace of life-giving repentance and deepen the reality of our dependence on God's merciful Fatherhood. So throughout this week, we will alternate between looking at our dignity as children of God and looking at how we are still little and being formed in the womb of Mary.

Sharing Christ's Sonship

Reading 1 *Galatians 4:4–7*

But when the time had fully come, God sent forth his Son, born of woman, born under the law, to redeem those who were under the law, so that we might receive adoption as sons. And because you are sons, God has sent the Spirit of his Son into our hearts, crying, "Abba! Father!" So through God you are no longer a slave but a son, and if a son then an heir.

Reading 2 *Pope St. John Paul II's apostolic letter* Tertio millennio adveniente *(November 10, 1994), no. 8*

The religion which originates in the mystery of the Redemptive Incarnation, is the religion of *"dwelling in the heart of God,"* of sharing in God's very life. St. Paul speaks of this in the passage already quoted: "God has sent the Spirit of his Son into our hearts, crying, 'Abba! Father!'" (Gal. 4:6). Man cries out like Christ Himself, who turned to God "with loud cries and tears" (Heb. 5:7), especially in Gethsemane and on the Cross: man cries out to God just as Christ cried out to Him, and thus he bears witness that he shares in Christ's Sonship through the power of the Holy Spirit. The Holy Spirit, whom the Father has sent in the name of the Son, enables man to share in the inmost life of God. He also enables man *to be a son, in the likeness of Christ*, and an heir of all that belongs to the Son (cf. Gal. 4:7). In this consists the religion of "dwelling in the inmost life of God," which begins with the Incarnation of the Son of God. The Holy Spirit, who searches the depths of God (cf. 1 Cor. 2:10), leads us, all mankind, into these depths by virtue of the sacrifice of Christ.

Reflection

The great dignity that Christ has given us is that we can share in the inmost life of God by sharing in Christ's Sonship. As we practice the religion of dwelling in the heart of God, we must remember that the heart of God once dwelled in the womb of Mary: indeed, the Son of God is also the Son of Mary. We are able to understand His Sonship, and thus also ours, by going back to the starting point of the God-Man in the womb of Mary. There we can allow ourselves to be formed by the Holy Spirit, the artisan of the Incarnation. There we can discover that we have an Eternal Father in God and a tender Mother in Mary. This relationship is our foundation, our starting point, and our identity. It does not depend on our accomplishments; we have done nothing to earn it, and no one can take it away from us. Like a baby in the womb, our share in Christ's Sonship is pure gift. We can only receive it and choose to keep growing as the little children of Mary God has called us to be.

Prayers

Ave Maris Stella or Sub Tuum Praesidium
Thomistic Litany of Humility
Litany of the Holy Spirit
Prayer of Entrustment to the Womb of Mary

Remaining Little

Reading 1 *Matthew 18:1–4*

At that time the disciples came to Jesus, saying, "Who is the greatest in the kingdom of heaven?" And calling to him a child, he put him in the midst of them, and said, "Truly, I say to you, unless you turn and become like children, you will never enter the kingdom of heaven. Whoever humbles himself like this child, he is the greatest in the kingdom of heaven."

Reading 2 *St. Thérèse of Lisieux*

St. Thérèse of Lisieux was asked on her deathbed what it means to "remain little," and she replied:

It is to recognize our nothingness, to expect everything from God as a little child expects everything from her father; it is to be disquieted about nothing, and not to be set on making our [own] living. Even among the poor, they give the child what is necessary, but as soon as she grows up, her father no longer wants to feed her and says: "Work now, you can take care of yourself."

It was so as not to hear this that I never wanted to grow up, feeling that I was incapable of making my [own] living, the eternal life of Heaven.

To be little is not attributing to oneself the virtues that one practices, believing oneself capable of anything, but recognizing that God places this treasure in the hands of His little child to be used when necessary; but it remains always God's treasure. Finally, it is not to become discouraged over one's faults, for children fall often, but they are too little to hurt themselves very much.[3]

Reflection

How do I view myself? Am I impressed with my virtues, accomplishments, skills, gifts, degrees, salary, moral perfection, knowledge, or eloquence of speech? Do I recognize that I have received everything I have—even my own life, my own being? Do I get discouraged over my faults? Do I beat myself up when I fail, or do I cast myself into the hands of God, trusting in the infinite love of my Heavenly Father? Do I allow my failures to remind me that I am simply a little child in Mary's womb, still developing with a long way to go?

Remember today that you were already loved before you ever accomplished anything. God loved you into existence and knowing that you would always need help, He gave you a Mother to take care of you. When you feel your littleness today, in weakness and failure, renew your decision to remain in the loving security of the womb of Mary.

Prayers

Ave Maris Stella or Sub Tuum Praesidium
Thomistic Litany of Humility
Litany of the Holy Spirit
Prayer of Entrustment to the Womb of Mary

---

[3] St. *Thérèse of Lisieux, Her Last Conversations*, trans. John Clarke (Washington, D.C.: ICS Publications, 1977), 138–139.

Not Judging

Reading 1 *James 4:6–12*

"God opposes the proud, but gives grace to the humble." Submit yourselves therefore to God. Resist the devil and he will flee from you. Draw near to God and he will draw near to you. Cleanse your hands, you sinners, and purify your hearts, you men of double mind. Be wretched and mourn and weep. Let your laughter be turned to mourning and your joy to dejection. Humble yourselves before the Lord and he will exalt you.

Do not speak evil against one another, brethren. He that speaks evil against a brother or judges his brother, speaks evil against the law, and judges the law. But if you judge the law, you are not a doer of the law but a judge. There is one lawgiver and judge, he who is able to save and to destroy. But who are you that you judge your neighbor?

Reading 2 *St. Dorotheos of Gaza*

If we have true love with sympathy and patient labor, we shall not go about scrutinizing our neighbor's shortcomings. As it is said, "Love covers up a multitude of sins," and again, "Love thinks no evil ... hides everything," etc. As I said, if we have true love, that very love should screen anything of this kind, as

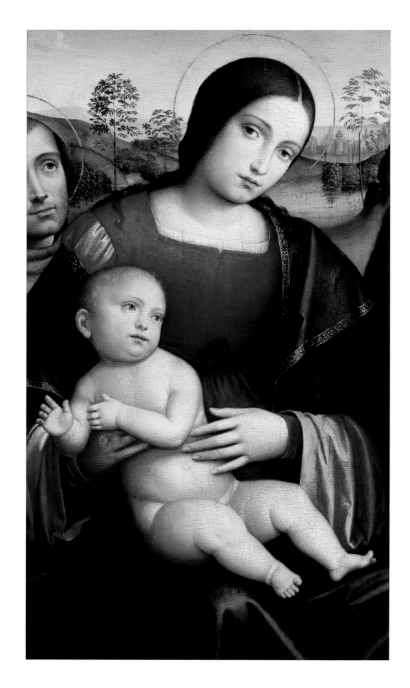

did the saints when they saw the shortcomings of men. Were they blind? Not at all! But they simply would not let their eyes dwell on sins. Who hated sin more than the saints? But they did not hate the sinners at the same time, nor condemn them, nor turn away from them, but they suffered with them, admonished them, comforted them, gave them remedies as sickly members, and did all they could to heal them.

Take a fisherman: when he casts his hook into the sea and a large fish takes the bait, he perceives first that the fish struggles violently and is full of fight, so he does not try to pull it in immediately by main force, for the line would break and the catch would be lost in the end. No! He plays out the line and, as he says, allows the fish to run freely, but when he feels the line slacken and the first struggles have calmed down, he takes up the slack line and begins, little by little, to draw him in. So the holy fathers, by patience and love, draw the brother and do not spurn him nor show themselves unfriendly towards him, but as a mother who has an unruly son does not hate him or turn away from him but rules him with sweetness and sometimes does things to please him, so they always protect him and keep him in order, and they gain a hold on him so that, with time, they correct the erring brother and do not allow him to harm anyone else, and in doing so they greatly advance towards the love of Christ.

What did the blessed Ammon do when those brothers, greatly disturbed, came to him and said, "Come and see, Father. There is a young woman in Brother X's cell!" What tenderness he showed to the erring brother. What great love there was in that great soul. Knowing that the brother had hidden the woman in a large barrel, he went in, sat down on it, and told the others to search the whole place. And when they found nothing, he said to them, "May God forgive you!" And so dismissing them in disgrace, he called out to them that they should not readily believe anything against their neighbor. By his consideration for his brother, he not only protected him after God but corrected him when the right moment came. For when they were alone, he laid on him the hand with which he had thrown the others out, and said, "Have a care for yourself, brother." Immediately, the other's conscience pricked him and he was stricken with remorse, so swiftly did the mercy and sympathy of the old man work upon his soul.

Let us, therefore, strive to gain this love for ourselves, let us acquire this tenderness towards our neighbor so that we may guard ourselves from wickedly speaking evil of our neighbor and from judging and despising him. Let us help one another, as we are members one of another. Which of us, having a wound on his hand or foot, or any other member, would despise it and cut it off, even if it turned septic? Would he not rather bathe it and take away the poison and put a plaster on it, sign it with the cross, apply a relic, and pray and beg the saints to pray for its cure?[4]

Reflection

Do I put myself in judgment over others? Do I presume to know what is happening in the heart of my brothers and sisters? Do I presume to know their motives and intentions? Do I know the degree of their freedom or the grace they are receiving? Do I choose to chastise rather than to pray? Do I rush to condemn rather than to overlook the sin for now? Do I entice others to forgiveness through mercy?

Mary takes all sinners into her womb and loves them. She realizes that we are all small and not yet fully formed. She chooses

---

[4] *Dorotheos of Gaza: Discourses and Sayings,* trans. Eric P. Wheeler (Kalamazoo, MI: Cistercian Publications, 1977), 136–138.

to nourish us and love us rather than to condemn us or abandon us. Let us pray that she may teach us to treat others with the same love and mercy.

Prayers

Ave Maris Stella or Sub Tuum Praesidium
Thomistic Litany of Humility
Litany of the Holy Spirit
Prayer of Entrustment to the Womb of Mary

Beloved Sinners: A Dignified Embarrassment

Reading 1

Luke 15:11–24

There was a man who had two sons; and the younger of them said to his father, "Father, give me the share of property that falls to me." And he divided his living between them. Not many days later, the younger son gathered all he had and took his journey into a far country, and there he squandered his property in loose living. And when he had spent everything, a great famine arose in that country, and he began to be in want. So he went and joined himself to one of the citizens of that country, who sent him into his fields to feed swine. And he would gladly have fed on the pods that the swine ate; and no one gave him anything. But when he came to himself he said, "How many of my father's hired servants have bread enough and to spare, but I perish here with hunger! I will arise and go to my father, and I will say to him, 'Father, I have sinned against heaven and before you; I am no longer worthy to be called your son; treat me as one of your hired servants.'" And he arose and came to his father. But while he was yet at a distance, his father saw him and had compassion, and ran and embraced him and kissed him. And the son said to him, "Father, I have sinned against heaven and before you; I am no longer worthy to be called your son." But the father said to his servants, "Bring quickly the best robe, and put it on him; and put a ring on his hand, and shoes on his feet; and bring the fatted calf and kill it, and let us eat and make merry; for this my son was dead, and is alive again; he was lost, and is found." And they began to make merry.

Reading 2

*Pope Francis's Retreat
Meditation, June 2, 2016*

Let us think for a moment about the "embarrassed dignity" of this prodigal yet beloved son. If we can serenely keep our heart balanced between those two extremes—dignity and embarrassment—without letting go of either of them, perhaps we can feel how the heart of our Father beats with love for us. It was a heart beating with worry, as he went up onto the roof to look out. What was he looking at? The possible return of his son.... In that moment, in that place where dignity and embarrassment exist side by side, we can perceive how our Father's heart beats. We can imagine that mercy wells up in it like blood. He goes out to seek us sinners. He draws us to Himself, purifies us, and sends us forth, new and renewed, to every periphery, to bring mercy to all. That blood is the Blood of Christ, the Blood of the new and eternal covenant of mercy, poured out for us and for all, for the forgiveness of sins. We contemplate that Blood by going in and out of His heart and the heart of the Father. That is our sole treasure, the only thing we have to give to the world: the Blood that purifies and brings peace to every reality and all people. The Blood of the Lord that forgives sins. The Blood that is true drink, for it reawakens and revives what was dead from sin.

In our serene prayer, which wavers between embarrassment and dignity, dignity and embarrassment, both together, let us ask for the grace to sense that mercy as giving meaning to our entire life, the grace to feel how the heart of the Father beats as one with our own. It is not enough to think of that grace as something God offers us from time to time, whenever He forgives some big sin of ours, so that then we can go off to do the rest by ourselves, alone. It is not enough.... The important thing is that each of us feel that fruitful tension born of the Lord's mercy: we are at one and the same time sinners pardoned and sinners restored to dignity. The Lord not only cleanses us but crowns us, giving us dignity.

Reflection

Pope Francis wrote earlier in that same meditation, "Mercy, seen in feminine terms, is the tender love of a mother who, touched by the frailty of her newborn baby, takes the child into her arms and provides everything it needs to live and grow (*rahamim*)." That Hebrew word, *rahamim*, is closely related to the Hebrew word for womb, *rehem*.

Learning to balance embarrassment and dignity is another way of describing how we remain in the womb of Mary. We are very small in her womb, and we feel how underdeveloped and incapable we are. At the same time, we are in the Seat of Wisdom, and we share a home with the Almighty Lord, Jesus Christ, as we are being formed into His likeness. We are embarrassed by our weakness, but we are also dignified in the nobility God freely gives us—wrapped in His royal robe and wearing the ring of His royal dignity.

Imagine yourself today like a little child, placed by Christ the King on His magnificent throne. Let yourself feel how tiny you are, in your limitations and even in your past sins, while at the same time feeling how loved and dignified you are sitting on that royal throne, which is also the lap of Mary.

Prayers

Ave Maris Stella or Sub Tuum Praesidium
Thomistic Litany of Humility
Litany of the Holy Spirit
Prayer of Entrustment to the Womb of Mary

Pastoral Acedia

Reading 1
Philippians 4:4–7

Rejoice in the Lord always; again I will say, Rejoice. Let all men know your forbearance. The Lord is at hand. Have no anxiety about anything, but in everything by prayer and supplication with thanksgiving let your requests be made known to God. And the peace of God, which passes all understanding, will keep your hearts and your minds in Christ Jesus.

Reading 2
Pope Francis's apostolic exhortation
Evangelii gaudium
(November 24, 2013), nos. 81–83

At a time when we most need a missionary dynamism which will bring salt and light to the world, many lay people fear that they may be asked to undertake some apostolic work, and they seek to avoid any responsibility that may take away from their free time. For example, it has become very difficult today to find trained parish catechists willing to persevere in this work for some years. Something similar is also happening with priests who are obsessed with protecting their free time. This is frequently due to the fact that people feel an overbearing need to guard their personal freedom, as though the task of evangelization was a dangerous poison rather than a joyful response to God's love which summons us to mission and makes us fulfilled and productive. Some resist giving themselves over completely to mission and thus end up in a state of paralysis and acedia.

The problem is not always an excess of activity but rather activity undertaken badly, without adequate motivation, without a spirituality which would permeate it and make it pleasurable. As a result, work becomes more tiring than necessary, even leading at times to illness. Far from a content and happy tiredness, this is a tense, burdensome, dissatisfying and, in the end, unbearable fatigue. This pastoral acedia can be caused by a number of things. Some fall into it because they throw themselves into unrealistic projects and are not satisfied simply to do what they reasonably can. Others, because they lack the patience to allow processes to mature; they want everything to fall from Heaven. Others, because they are attached to a few projects or vain dreams of success. Others, because they have lost real contact with people and so depersonalize their work that they are more concerned with the road map than with the journey itself. Others fall into acedia because they are unable to wait; they want to dominate the rhythm of life. Today's obsession with immediate results makes it hard for pastoral workers to tolerate anything that smacks of disagreement, possible failure, criticism, the cross.

And so the biggest threat of all gradually takes shape: "the gray pragmatism of the daily life of the Church, in which all appears to proceed normally, while in reality faith is wearing down and degenerating into small-mindedness." A tomb psychology thus develops and slowly transforms Christians into mummies in a museum. Disillusioned with reality, with the Church and with themselves, they experience a constant temptation to cling to a faint melancholy, lacking in hope, which seizes the heart like "the most precious of the devil's potions." Called to radiate light and communicate life, in the end they are caught up in things that generate only darkness and inner weariness, and slowly

consume all zeal for the apostolate. For all this, I repeat: Let us not allow ourselves to be robbed of the joy of evangelization!

Reflection

Do I fearfully guard my free time? Am I afraid of being asked to give too much? Have I lost the joy of the gospel and the joy of sharing the gospel? Have I become disillusioned with the Church, with my ministry, with others, or with myself?

Sometimes we settle for that which we believe we can accomplish on our own, but when we set our sights too low, we quickly lose inspiration and motivation. Other times, we may feel overwhelmed because we are trying to do everything alone. But either way, we must remember that we are not alone! Although we are very small, with Mary's help, by the grace of God, we truly can do great things. In fact, if we remain in Mary's womb, we let her do great things through us and consent to do them with her, just like Jesus did when Mary took Him to greet her cousin Elizabeth.

Are we willing to accept whatever Mary wants to do with us to spread the gospel and bring good news to the poor?

Prayers

Ave Maris Stella or Sub Tuum Praesidium
Thomistic Litany of Humility
Litany of the Holy Spirit
Prayer of Entrustment to the Womb of Mary

Christian "Diseases"

Reading 1
Luke 12:16–21

He told them a parable, saying, "The land of a rich man brought forth plentifully; and he thought to himself, 'What shall I do, for I have nowhere to store my crops?' And he said, 'I will do this: I will pull down my barns, and build larger ones; and there I will store all my grain and my goods. And I will say to my soul, Soul, you have ample goods laid up for many years; take your ease, eat, drink, be merry.' But God said to him, 'Fool! This night your soul is required of you; and the things you have prepared, whose will they be?' So is he who lays up treasure for himself, and is not rich toward God."

Reading 2
Pope Francis's Address to the Roman Curia, December 22, 2014

The Curia is called constantly to improve and to grow in communion, holiness, and wisdom, in order to carry out fully its mission. And yet, like any body, like any human body, it is also exposed to diseases, malfunctioning, infirmity. Here I would like to mention some of these probable diseases, "curial diseases" ... which weaken our service to the Lord. ...

[One is] the disease of thinking we are "immortal," "immune," or downright "indispensable," neglecting the need for

regular check-ups. A Curia which is not *self-critical*, which does not keep up with things, which does not seek to be more fit, is a sick body. A simple visit to the cemetery might help us see the names of many people who thought they were immortal, immune, and indispensable! It is the disease of the rich fool in the Gospel, who thought he would live forever (cf. Luke 12:13–21), but also of those who turn into lords and masters and think of themselves as above others and not at their service. It is often an effect of the pathology of power, from a superiority complex, from a narcissism which passionately gazes at its own image and does not see the image of God on the face of others, especially the weakest and those most in need. The antidote to this plague is the grace of realizing that we are sinners and able to say heartily: "We are unworthy servants. We have only done what was our duty" (Luke 17:10).

Another disease is the "Martha complex," excessive busyness. It is found in those who immerse themselves in work and inevitably neglect "the better part": sitting at the feet of Jesus (cf. Luke 10:38-42). Jesus called His disciples to "rest a while" (cf. Mark 6:31) for a reason, because neglecting needed rest leads to stress and agitation. A time of rest, for those who have completed their work, is necessary, obligatory, and should be taken seriously: by spending time with one's family and respecting holidays as moments of spiritual and physical recharging. We need to learn from Qohelet that "for everything there is a season" (Eccles. 3:1-15)....

[There is also] the disease of gossiping, grumbling, and backbiting. I have already spoken many times about this disease, but never enough. It is a grave illness that begins simply, perhaps even in small talk, and takes over a person, making him become a "sower of weeds" (like Satan) and, in many cases, a cold-blooded killer of the good name of our colleagues and confrères. It is the disease of cowardly persons who lack the courage to speak out directly but instead speak behind other people's backs. St. Paul admonishes us to "do all things without grumbling or questioning, that you may be blameless and innocent" (Phil. 2:14-15). Brothers, let us be on our guard against the terrorism of gossip!

Reflection

We can see how dangerous these "diseases" are when we see that we are in the womb of Mary. When we introduce diseases into the womb, we make that environment toxic, and it poisons ourselves as well as others. These diseases damage our own growth as well as the growth of others, and if they become serious enough, they can cause a kind of spiritual miscarriage.

Boasting about our importance can be quickly corrected by remembering that we are infants in the womb. We are not that impressive, we are completely dependent on Mary, and we are certainly no more important than all our twins who share the womb with us. Likewise, we can understand how very ridiculous the idolatry of the "Martha Complex" is when we realize how limited we are in the womb of Mary. Consider, too, how the toxicity of gossip raises the pH in the womb to dangerous levels and stunts our growth. We can feel the poison of negativity in the amniotic fluid in which we are swimming.

Am I impressed with myself? Do I think I am immortal or irreplaceable? Do I work too much, and does this excess in my work cause me to neglect prayer and proper rest? Do I engage in the terrorism of gossip and make comments that destroy the reputation of others?

Let us become little and accept our beloved insignificance in the womb of Mary—our lives may not matter much to the world, but they matter tremendously to our Mother!

Prayers

Ave Maris Stella or Sub Tuum Praesidium
Thomistic Litany of Humility
Litany of the Holy Spirit
Prayer of Entrustment to the Womb of Mary

Called to Holiness

Reading 1 *1 Thessalonians 4:1–8*

Finally, brethren, we beg and exhort you in the Lord Jesus, that as you learned from us how you ought to walk and to please God, just as you are doing, you do so more and more. For you know what instructions we gave you through the Lord Jesus. For this is the will of God, your sanctification: that you abstain from immorality; that each one of you know how to control his own body in holiness and honor, not in the passion of lust like heathens who do not know God; that no man transgress, and wrong his brother in this matter, because the Lord is an avenger in all these things, as we solemnly forewarned you. For God has not called us for uncleanness, but in holiness. Therefore whoever disregards this, disregards not man but God, who gives his Holy Spirit to you.

Reading 2 *Pope St. John Paul II's apostolic letter*
Novo millennio ineunte
(January 6, 2001), nos. 30–32

It is necessary ... to rediscover the full practical significance of chapter 5 of the Dogmatic Constitution on the Church *Lumen Gentium*, dedicated to the "universal call to holiness." The

Council Fathers laid such stress on this point, not just to embellish ecclesiology with a kind of spiritual veneer, but to make the call to holiness an intrinsic and essential aspect of their teaching on the Church. The rediscovery of the Church as "mystery," or as a people "gathered together by the unity of the Father, the Son, and the Holy Spirit," was bound to bring with it a rediscovery of the Church's "holiness," understood in the basic sense of belonging to Him who is in essence the Holy One, the "thrice Holy" (cf. Isa. 6:3). To profess the Church as holy means to point to her as the Bride of Christ, for whom He gave Himself precisely in order to make her holy (cf. Eph. 5:25–26). This, as it were, objective gift of holiness is offered to all the baptized.

But the gift in turn becomes a task, which must shape the whole of Christian life: "This is the will of God, your sanctification" (1 Thess. 4:3). It is a duty which concerns not only certain Christians: "All the Christian faithful, of whatever state or rank, are called to the fullness of the Christian life and to the perfection of charity."

… Since Baptism is a true entry into the holiness of God through incorporation into Christ and the indwelling of His Spirit, it would be a contradiction to settle for a life of mediocrity, marked by a minimalist ethic and a shallow religiosity.…

As the Council itself explained, this ideal of perfection must not be misunderstood as if it involved some kind of extraordinary existence, possible only for a few "uncommon heroes" of holiness. The ways of holiness are many, according to the vocation of each individual. I thank the Lord that in these years He has enabled me to beatify and canonize a large number of Christians, and among them many lay people who attained holiness in the most ordinary circumstances of life. The time has come to repropose wholeheartedly to everyone this *high standard of ordinary Christian living*: the whole life of the Christian community and of Christian families must lead in this direction. It is also clear, however, that the paths to holiness are personal and call for a genuine *"training in holiness,"* adapted to people's needs.... This training in holiness calls for a Christian life distinguished above all in *the art of prayer.*

Reflection

"Baptism is a true entry into the holiness of God," and Baptism is also an immersion into the womb of Mary. All who are in her womb are given all they need to become holy.

Holiness involves letting ourselves be formed into the likeness of Christ in the womb of Mary. We do everything with her. The "high standard of ordinary Christian living" can often seem daunting, but it becomes so much easier when we realize that we simply need to remain with our Mother and let her form us in holiness into her Son.

Mary is making you a saint just by loving you. Are you letting her love you, care for you, form you? When you get overwhelmed by the high standard of ordinary Christian living, do you seek refuge in the womb of Mary? Like a good mother, Mary teaches us the art of prayer. Do you look to her in order to learn how to pray? Let us acknowledge our littleness and entrust ourselves to Mary's womb so that she can form us in holiness.

Prayers

> Ave Maris Stella or Sub Tuum Praesidium
> Thomistic Litany of Humility
> Litany of the Holy Spirit
> Prayer of Entrustment to the Womb of Mary

Week of Knowledge
of Mary

❖

Introduction

❖

Reading

Pope St. John Paul II's apostolic letter
Rosarium virginis mariae
(October 16, 2002), no. 14

Christ is the supreme Teacher, the revealer and the one revealed. It is not just a question of learning what He taught but of "*learning Him.*" In this regard, could we have any better teacher than Mary? From the divine standpoint, the Spirit is the interior teacher who leads us to the full truth of Christ (cf. John 14:26; 15:26; 16:13). But among creatures, no one knows Christ better than Mary; no one can introduce us to a profound knowledge of His mystery better than His Mother.

The first of the "signs" worked by Jesus—the changing of water into wine at the marriage in Cana—clearly presents Mary in the guise of a teacher, as she urges the servants to do what Jesus commands (cf. John 2:5). We can imagine that she would have done likewise for the disciples after Jesus' Ascension, when she joined them in awaiting the Holy Spirit and supported them in their first mission. Contemplating the scenes of the Rosary in union with Mary is a means of learning from her to "read" Christ, to discover His secrets and to understand His message.

This school of Mary is all the more effective if we consider that she teaches by obtaining for us in abundance the gifts of the Holy Spirit, even as she offers us the incomparable example of her own "pilgrimage of faith." As we contemplate each mystery of her Son's life, she invites us to do as she did at the Annunciation: to ask humbly the questions which open us to the light, in order to end with the obedience of faith: "Behold I am the handmaid of the Lord; be it done to me according to your word" (Luke 1:38).

Reflection

As we set out on this next week of preparation, we shift our gaze to Mary, our Mother and teacher, and we learn from her, particularly by meditating with her and in her on the mysteries of the Rosary. Praying the Rosary is an essential part of this week of preparation and an essential part of living in the womb of Mary, where we are formed into the full maturity of Christ.

While we pray the Rosary and meditate on the lives of Jesus and Mary, we should remember that we will also need the gifts of the Holy Spirit as we prepare for our consecration. The gifts of the Holy Spirit are essentially the qualities of Christ (His Wisdom, His Knowledge, His Fortitude, etc.), and they are woven into the heart and soul of the one who is formed in Mary's womb. Let us continue to ask the Holy Spirit each day for His sevenfold gift so that He might shape us into Christ in the womb of Mary.

The Rosary Helps Consecrate Us to Mary

Reading 1

Galatians 4:18–19

For a good purpose it is always good to be made much of, and not only when I am present with you. My little children, with whom I am again in travail until Christ be formed in you!

Reading 2

Pope St. John Paul II's apostolic letter
Rosarium virginis mariae, *no. 15*

Christian spirituality is distinguished by the disciple's commitment to become conformed ever more fully to his Master (cf. Rom. 8:29; Phil. 3:10, 12). The outpouring of the Holy Spirit in Baptism grafts the believer like a branch onto the vine which is Christ (cf. John 15:5) and makes him a member of Christ's mystical Body (cf. 1 Cor. 12:12; Rom. 12:5). This initial unity, however, calls for a growing assimilation which will increasingly shape the conduct of the disciple in accordance with the "mind" of Christ: "Have this mind among yourselves, which was in Christ Jesus" (Phil. 2:5). In the words of the Apostle, we are called "to put on the Lord Jesus Christ" (cf. Rom. 13:14; Gal. 3:27).

In the spiritual journey of the Rosary, based on the constant contemplation—in Mary's company—of the face of Christ, this demanding ideal of being conformed to Him is pursued through an association which could be described in terms of friendship. We are thereby enabled to enter naturally into Christ's life and as it were to share His deepest feelings. In this regard, Bl. Bartolo Longo has written: "Just as two friends, frequently in each other's company, tend to develop similar habits, so too, by holding familiar converse with Jesus and the Blessed Virgin, by meditating on the mysteries of the Rosary and by living the same life in Holy communion, we can become, to the extent of our lowliness, similar to them and can learn from these supreme models a life of humility, poverty, hiddenness, patience, and perfection" (*I Quindici Sabati del Santissimo Rosario*, 27th ed. [Pompei, 1916], 27).

In this process of being conformed to Christ in the Rosary, we entrust ourselves in a special way to the maternal care of the Blessed Virgin. She who is both the Mother of Christ and a member of the Church, indeed her "pre-eminent and altogether singular member" (*Lumen Gentium*, no. 53), is at the same time the "Mother of the Church." As such, she continually brings to birth children for the mystical Body of her Son. She does so through her intercession, imploring upon them the inexhaustible outpouring of the Spirit. Mary is *the perfect icon of the motherhood of the Church.*

The Rosary mystically transports us to Mary's side as she is busy watching over the human growth of Christ in the home of Nazareth. This enables her to train us and to mold us with the same care, until Christ is "fully formed" in us (cf. Gal. 4:19). This role of Mary, totally grounded in that of Christ and radically subordinated to it, "in no way obscures or diminishes the unique mediation of Christ, but rather shows its power" (*Lumen Gentium*, no. 60). This is the luminous principle expressed by the Second Vatican Council which I have so powerfully experienced

in my own life and have made the basis of my episcopal motto: *Totus Tuus* (cf. First Radio Address *Urbi et Orbi* (17 October 1978): AAS 70 (1978), 927). The motto is of course inspired by the teaching of St. Louis-Marie Grignion de Montfort, who explained in the following words Mary's role in the process of our configuration to Christ: "*Our entire perfection consists in being conformed, united, and consecrated to Jesus Christ. Hence the most* perfect of all devotions is undoubtedly that which conforms, unites, and consecrates us most perfectly to Jesus Christ. Now, since Mary is of all creatures the one most conformed to Jesus Christ, it follows that among all devotions that which most consecrates and conforms a soul to our Lord is devotion to Mary, His Holy Mother, and that the more a soul is consecrated to her the more will it be consecrated to Jesus Christ" (*Treatise on True Devotion to the Blessed Virgin Mary*). Never as in the Rosary do the life of Jesus and that of Mary appear so deeply joined. Mary lives only in Christ and for Christ!

Reflection

"The Rosary mystically transports us to Mary's side." Is there ever a time that we do not need to be at Mary's side? We are like babies in the womb who need constant support, nourishment, love, and protection from our Mother. Is our life ever made better by being away from Mary? As Pope St. John Paul II taught us, when we are at Mary's side, she will always train us and mold us until Christ is fully formed in us. Even as we simply hold the beads of the Rosary, we hold Mary's hand. By contemplating Christ with Mary as we pray the Rosary, "we are thereby enabled to enter naturally into Christ's life and as it were to share His deepest feelings."

Let us enter into this adventure of discovery, exploring the interior life of Christ through contemplating His Mysteries with Mary as we pray the Rosary.

Prayers

Litany of the Holy Spirit or Veni Sancte Spiritus
Rosary (or at least one decade), followed by the
    Litany of Loreto
Prayer of Entrustment to the Womb of Mary

Mary, Abandoned to God, Becomes Our Mother

Reading 1

Luke 1:26–38

In the sixth month the angel Gabriel was sent from God to a city of Galilee named Nazareth, to a virgin betrothed to a man whose name was Joseph, of the house of David; and the virgin's name was Mary. And he came to her and said, "Hail, full of grace, the Lord is with you!" But she was greatly troubled at the saying, and considered in her mind what sort of greeting this might be. And the angel said to her, "Do not be afraid, Mary, for you have found favor with God. And behold, you will conceive in your womb and bear a son, and you shall call his name Jesus. He will be great, and will be called the Son of the Most High; and the Lord God will give to him the throne of his father David, and he will reign over the house of Jacob forever; and of his kingdom there will be no end."

And Mary said to the angel, "How can this be, since I have no husband?" And the angel said to her, "The Holy Spirit will come upon you, and the power of the Most High will overshadow you; therefore the child to be born will be called holy, the Son of God.

And behold, your kinswoman Elizabeth in her old age has also conceived a son; and this is the sixth month with her who was called barren. For with God nothing will be impossible." And Mary said, "Behold, I am the handmaid of the Lord; let it be to me according to your word." And the angel departed from her.

Reading 2

Pope Benedict XVI's homily on the Solemnity of the Immaculate Conception, December 8, 2005

This is something we should indeed learn on the day of the Immaculate Conception: the person who abandons himself totally in God's hands does not become God's puppet, a boring "yes man"; he does not lose his freedom. Only the person who entrusts himself totally to God finds true freedom, the great, creative immensity of the freedom of good.

The person who turns to God does not become smaller but greater, for through God and with God he becomes great, he becomes divine, he becomes truly himself. The person who puts himself in God's hands does not distance himself from others, withdrawing into his private salvation; on the contrary, it is only then that his heart truly awakens and he becomes a sensitive, hence, benevolent and open person.

The closer a person is to God, the closer he is to people. We see this in Mary. The fact that she is totally with God is the reason why she is so close to human beings.

For this reason she can be the Mother of every consolation and every help, a Mother whom anyone can dare to address in any kind of need in weakness and in sin, for she has understanding for everything and is for everyone the open power of creative goodness.

Mary thus stands before us as a sign of comfort, encouragement, and hope. She turns to us, saying: "Have the courage to

dare with God! Try it! Do not be afraid of Him! Have the courage to risk with faith! Have the courage to risk with goodness! Have the courage to risk with a pure heart! Commit yourselves to God, then you will see that it is precisely by doing so that your life will become broad and light, not boring but filled with infinite surprises, for God's infinite goodness is never depleted!"

... Let us thank the Lord for the great sign of His goodness which He has given us in Mary, His Mother and the Mother of the Church. Let us pray to Him to put Mary on our path like a light that also helps us to become a light and to carry this light into the nights of history. Amen.

Reflection

Pope Benedict XVI encourages us that by drawing closer to God we are not diminished by our dependence but rather strengthened, sanctified, and even divinized: "The person who turns to God does not become smaller but greater, for through God and with God he becomes great, he becomes divine, he becomes truly himself." When we are in the womb of Mary with Jesus, people can only see our beautiful, pregnant Mother, and they know that inside her is her divine Son. In other words, when they look at us, they see her and imagine Him.

It is a great risk to remain so little in her womb. In this world we feel vulnerable when we seek to live by faith, when we try to be good, and when we strive to have a pure heart. But it is a risk that opens us up to an adventure of infinite surprises. Mary will carry us into completely new places, and far beyond our own capacity. Along the way, we will develop her sensitivities and her charity in our relationships with others.

Do you want to live this adventure in littleness, or would you rather settle for a secure life under your own control? Will you take the risk of remaining in the womb of Mary? Will you let her purify your heart and help you to be good, or will you prefer the ways of the world? Let us take the risk of dependence on Mary, and have the courage to risk with faith, the courage to risk with goodness, the courage to risk with a pure heart! Let us commit ourselves to God!

Prayers

> Litany of the Holy Spirit or Veni Sancte Spiritus
> Rosary (or at least one decade), followed by the
>   Litany of Loreto
> Prayer of Entrustment to the Womb of Mary

The Weak Are Formed into Christ

Reading 1 *Ephesians 4:11–16*

And his gifts were that some should be apostles, some prophets, some evangelists, some pastors and teachers, for the equipment of the saints, for the work of ministry, for building up the body of Christ, until we all attain to the unity of the faith and of the knowledge of the Son of God, to mature manhood, to the measure of the stature of the fullness of Christ; so that we may no longer be children, tossed to and fro and carried about with every wind of doctrine, by the cunning of men, by their craftiness in deceitful wiles. Rather, speaking the truth in love, we are to grow up in every way into him who is the head, into Christ, from whom the whole body, joined and knit together by every joint with which it is supplied, when each part is working properly, makes bodily growth and upbuilds itself in love.

Reading 2 *St. Louis de Montfort's* The Secret of Mary, *nos. 14, 16–18*

Mary received from God a unique dominion over souls enabling her to nourish them and make them more and more godlike.

St. Augustine went so far as to say that even in this world all the elect are enclosed in the womb of Mary, and that their real birthday is when this good mother brings them forth to eternal life. Consequently, just as an infant draws all its nourishment from its mother, who gives according to its needs, so the elect draw their spiritual nourishment and all their strength from Mary....

Mary is called by St. Augustine, and is indeed, the "living mold of God." In her alone the God-Man was formed in His human nature without losing any feature of the Godhead. In her alone, by the grace of Jesus Christ, man is made godlike as far as human nature is capable of it.

A sculptor can make a statue or a life-like model in two ways: (i) By using his skill, strength, experience, and good tools to produce a statue out of hard, shapeless matter; (ii) By making a cast of it in a mold. The first way is long and involved and open to all sorts of accidents. It only needs a faulty stroke of the chisel or hammer to ruin the whole work. The second is quick, easy, straightforward, almost effortless, and inexpensive, but the mold must be perfect and true to life and the material must be easy to handle and offer no resistance.

Mary is the great mold of God, fashioned by the Holy Spirit to give human nature to a Man who is God by the hypostatic union, and to fashion through grace men who are like to God. No godly feature is missing from this mold. Everyone who casts himself into it and allows himself to be molded will acquire every feature of Jesus Christ, true God, with little pain or effort, as befits his weak human condition. He will take on a faithful likeness to Jesus with no possibility of distortion, for the devil has never had and never will have any access to Mary, the holy and immaculate Virgin, in whom there is not the least suspicion of a stain of sin.

Dear friend, what a difference there is between a soul brought up in the ordinary way to resemble Jesus Christ by people who, like sculptors, rely on their own skill and industry, and a soul thoroughly tractable, entirely detached, most ready to be molded in her by the working of the Holy Spirit. What blemishes and defects, what shadows and distortions, what natural and human imperfections are found in the first soul, and what a faithful and divine likeness to Jesus is found in the second!

Reflection

As the Fathers of the Church affirmed, God became man that man might become God. This is already an unbelievable gift, but we might be suspicious that this only applies to some men and women, perhaps only to the strong, to those who are nearly saints already. Our Catholic Christian tradition denounces that deception, however, and affirms that Christ came so that all might be saved and that all might grow up into Christ. St. Louis de Montfort elaborates on this sound doctrine and encourages us to see that weakness makes it even easier for us, because we are supernaturally drawn to the safest place, the womb of Mary. Furthermore, that womb is the most perfect place to be formed into Christ, because that is precisely the place that Christ was formed.

When we feel our weakness, our littleness, and our poverty, and when we are tempted to give up or get discouraged, we can find refuge and consolation in the womb of Mary. Then we can remember what St. Louis teaches us: Mary's womb is the best place to be formed perfectly into saints, into Christ Himself.

Prayers

Litany of the Holy Spirit or Veni Sancte Spiritus
Rosary (or at least one decade), followed by the
    Litany of Loreto
Prayer of Entrustment to the Womb of Mary

The Holy Name of Mary

Reading 1 *Luke 1:26–27*

In the sixth month the angel Gabriel was sent from God to a city of Galilee named Nazareth, to a virgin betrothed to a man whose name was Joseph, of the house of David; and the virgin's name was Mary.

Reading 2 *Homily of St. Bernard of Clairvaux, Abbot and Doctor*

This verse ends: "And the Virgin's name was Mary." Let us now say a few words about this name, which means "star of the sea" and is so becoming to the Virgin Mother. Surely she is very fittingly likened to a star. The star sends forth its ray without harm to itself. In the same way, the Virgin brought forth her Son with no injury to herself. The ray no more diminishes the star's brightness than does the Son His mother's integrity. She is indeed that noble star risen out of Jacob whose beam enlightens this earthly globe. She it is whose brightness both twinkles in the highest Heaven and pierces the pit of Hell, and is shed upon earth, warming our hearts far more than our

bodies, fostering virtue and cauterizing vice. She, I tell you, is that splendid and wondrous star suspended as by necessity over this great wide sea, radiant with merit and brilliant in example. O you, whoever you are, who feel that in the tidal wave of this world you are nearer to being tossed about among the squalls and gales than treading on dry land, if you do not want to founder in the tempest, do not avert your eyes from the brightness of this star. When the wind of temptation blows up within you, when you strike upon the rock of tribulation, gaze up at this star, call out to Mary. Whether you are being tossed about by the waves of pride or ambition or slander or jealousy, gaze up at this star, call out to Mary. When rage or greed or fleshly desires are battering the skiff of your soul, gaze up at Mary. When the immensity of your sins weighs you down and you are bewildered by the loathsomeness of your conscience, when the terrifying thought of judgment appalls you and you begin to founder in the gulf of sadness and despair, think of Mary. In dangers, in hardships, in every doubt, think of Mary, call out to Mary. Keep her in your mouth, keep her in your heart. Follow the example of her life, and you will obtain the favor of her prayer. Following her, you will never go astray. Asking her help, you will never despair. Keeping her in your thoughts, you will never wander away. With your hand in hers, you will never stumble. With her protecting you, you will not be afraid. With her leading you, you will never tire. Her kindness will see you through to the end. Then you will know by your own experience how true it is that "the Virgin's name was Mary."[5]

---

[5] Bernard of Clairvaux, *Homilies in Praise of the Blessed Virgin Mary*, trans. Marie-Bernard Saïd, vol. 18-A (Kalamazoo, MI: Cistercian Publications, 1993), 30–31.

Reflection

The first word many children speak is "Mama"; it is their name for their mother. As St. Bernard teaches us, our Mother's name is the word we must practice most while we are in the womb of Mary. It is in speaking her name that we will remain her little children, always crying out to our Mama. We need to practice saying her name and calling on her in our best times and in our worst times. When things go well, we know we have done everything in her, from her womb. When things go poorly, we know how much help we need, and we call on her to soothe our guilty conscience.

Let us think of those times when we are most tempted to despair, most prone to wander, most in danger of going astray, most lost, fearful, or weary. And let us practice saying her name, the name of Mary.

Prayers

Litany of the Holy Spirit or Veni Sancte Spiritus
Rosary (or at least one decade), followed by the
   Litany of Loreto
Prayer of Entrustment to the Womb of Mary

Mary and the Church

Reading 1 *John 19:25–28*

Standing by the cross of Jesus were his mother, and his mother's sister, Mary the wife of Clopas, and Mary Magdalene. When Jesus saw his mother, and the disciple whom he loved standing near, he said to his mother, "Woman, behold, your son!" Then he said to the disciple, "Behold, your mother!" And from that hour the disciple took her to his own home. After this Jesus, knowing that all was now finished, said (to fulfill the scripture), "I thirst."

Reading 2 *Pope Francis's apostolic exhortation*
Evangelii gaudium, nos. 285–286

On the Cross, when Jesus endured in His own flesh the dramatic encounter of the sin of the world and God's mercy, He could feel at His feet the consoling presence of His Mother and His friend. At that crucial moment, before fully accomplishing the work which His Father had entrusted to Him, Jesus said to Mary: "Woman, here is your son." Then He said to His beloved friend: "Here is your mother" (John 19:26-27). These words of the dying Jesus are not chiefly the expression of His devotion and concern for His Mother; rather, they are a revelatory formula which manifests the mystery of a special saving mission. Jesus left us His Mother to be our Mother. Only after doing so did Jesus know that "all was now finished" (John 19:28). At the foot of the Cross, at the supreme hour of the new creation, Christ led us to Mary. He brought us to her because He did not want us to journey without a mother, and our people read in this maternal image all the mysteries of the Gospel. The Lord did not want to leave the Church without this icon of womanhood. Mary, who brought Him into the world with great faith, also accompanies "the rest of her offspring, those who keep the commandments of God and bear testimony to Jesus" (Rev. 12:17). The close connection between Mary, the Church, and each member of the faithful, based on the fact that each in his or her own way brings forth Christ, has been beautifully expressed by Bl. Isaac of Stella: "In the inspired Scriptures, what is said in a universal sense of the virgin mother, the Church, is understood in an individual sense of the Virgin Mary.... In a way, every Christian is also believed to be a bride of God's word, a mother of Christ, His daughter and sister, at once virginal and fruitful.... Christ dwelt for nine months in the tabernacle of Mary's womb. He dwells until the end of the ages in the tabernacle of the Church's faith. He will dwell forever in the knowledge and love of each faithful soul" (Isaac of Stella, *Sermo* 51: PL 194, 1863, 1865).

Mary was able to turn a stable into a home for Jesus, with poor swaddling clothes and an abundance of love. She is the handmaid of the Father who sings His praises. She is the friend who is ever concerned that wine not be lacking in our lives. She is the woman whose heart was pierced by a sword and who understands all our pain.... As she did with Juan Diego, Mary offers [us] maternal comfort and love, and whispers in [our] ear: "Let your heart not be troubled.... Am I not here, who am your Mother?" (*Nican Mopohua*, 118-119).

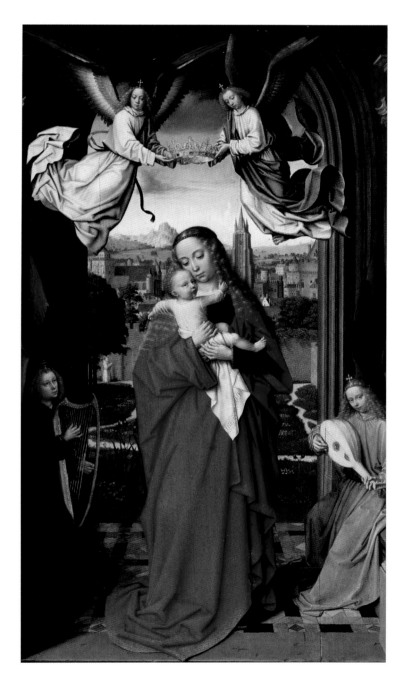

Reflection

After Jesus gave us His Mother to be our Mother, the Gospel says that He knew all was finished. He knew that we needed a perfect mother to help us make the journey of Christian faith. But Jesus, out of an abundance of love and concern, has actually given us two perfect Mothers: Mary and the Church.

Mary is able to turn the stable of our hearts into a home for Jesus, no matter how poor we feel we are. Likewise, since, as Bl. Isaac of Stella taught us, what we can say about Mary, we can say about the Church, the Church is the place of true liberation and healing, as the womb of Mary is the womb of the Church. Through Marian consecration, we come to see our relationship with the Church as being in the womb of our Mother, and we discover the consolation and transformation that come from being so rooted in grace and surrounded by prayer.

Where is the stable in your life that Mary can turn into a home? Where are the poor and hurting places in your heart that need a mother's tender care? Where do you feel joyless and need a friend to cheer you up? Let us acknowledge Mary as our Mother in the heart of Mother Church.

Prayers

Litany of the Holy Spirit or Veni Sancte Spiritus
Rosary (or at least one decade), followed by the
　　Litany of Loreto
Prayer of Entrustment to the Womb of Mary

Mary, Our Fiercely Compassionate Mother

Reading 1 *Luke 15:3–7*

So he told them this parable: "What man of you, having a hundred sheep, if he has lost one of them, does not leave the ninety-nine in the wilderness, and go after the one which is lost, until he finds it? And when he has found it, he lays it on his shoulders, rejoicing. And when he comes home, he calls together his friends and his neighbors, saying to them, 'Rejoice with me, for I have found my sheep which was lost.' Just so, I tell you, there will be more joy in heaven over one sinner who repents than over ninety-nine righteous persons who need no repentance."

Reading 2 *Pope Benedict XVI's homily on the Solemnity of the Immaculate Conception, December 8, 2005*

In her, God has impressed His own image, the image of the One who follows the lost sheep even up into the mountains and among the briars and thornbushes of the sins of this world, letting Himself be spiked by the crown of thorns of these sins in order to take the sheep on His shoulders and bring it home.

As a merciful Mother, Mary is the anticipated figure and everlasting portrait of the Son. Thus, we see that the image of the Sorrowful Virgin, of the Mother who shares her suffering and her love, is also a true image of the Immaculate Conception. Her heart was enlarged by being and feeling together with God. In her, God's goodness came very close to us.

Reflection

We know how fiercely a mother will fight, suffer, and put herself in harm's way in order to protect her children. Think of the saintly mothers throughout history who have gone so far as to lay down their lives to protect their babies in the womb, such as St. Gianna Beretta Molla and Servant of God Chiara Corbella Petrillo.

Our Mother Mary loves us even more than these mothers, though. When we are in the womb of Mary, there is no pain or threat we face that she does not share with us. Her fiercely maternal heart shares in our sorrows, and she will never abandon us, no matter what the cost to her might be.

Turn to Mary in times of sorrow, mourning, and suffering. The Queen of Sorrows feels our pain and will comfort us as we take solace in her loving womb.

Prayers

Litany of the Holy Spirit or Veni Sancte Spiritus
Rosary (or at least one decade), followed by the
Litany of Loreto
Prayer of Entrustment to the Womb of Mary

Mary, Our Refuge

Reading 1 *Revelation 12:1–6*

And a great portent appeared in heaven, a woman clothed with the sun, with the moon under her feet, and on her head a crown of twelve stars; she was with child and she cried out in her pangs of birth, in anguish for delivery. And another portent appeared in heaven; behold, a great red dragon, with seven heads and ten horns, and seven diadems upon his heads. His tail swept down a third of the stars of heaven, and cast them to the earth. And the dragon stood before the woman who was about to bear a child, that he might devour her child when she brought it forth; she brought forth a male child, one who is to rule all the nations with a rod of iron, but her child was caught up to God and to his throne, and the woman fled into the wilderness, where she has a place prepared by God, in which to be nourished for one thousand two hundred and sixty days.

Reading 2 *Pope Francis's homily for a Mass for the Translation of the Miraculous Image of Mary* Salus Populi Romani, *January 28, 2018*

The Christian people have understood, from the very beginning, that in difficulties and trials we need to turn to our Mother, as

the most ancient Marian hymn has it: *Beneath your protection, we seek refuge, O Holy Mother of God; do not despise our petitions in our necessities, but deliver us always from all dangers, O Glorious and Blessed Virgin. Amen.*

We seek refuge. Our fathers in faith taught that in turbulent moments we should gather under the mantle of the Holy Mother of God. At one time those who were persecuted and in need sought refuge with high-ranking noble women: when their cloak, regarded as inviolable, was held out as a sign of welcoming, protection had been granted. So it is for us with regard to Our Lady, the highest woman of the human race. Her mantle is always open to receive us and gather us. The Christian East reminds us of this, where many celebrate the Protection of the Mother of God, who in a beautiful icon is depicted with her mantle sheltering her sons and daughters and covering the whole world. Monks of old recommended, in times of trial, that we take refuge beneath the mantle of the Holy Mother of God: calling upon her as "Holy Mother of God" was already a guarantee of protection and help, this prayer over and again: "Holy Mother of God," "Holy Mother of God" — just like this.

This wisdom, that comes to us from far off, helps us: the Mother protects the faith, safeguards relationships, saves those in storms, and preserves them from evil. Where our Mother is at home, the devil does not enter in. Where our Mother is at home, the devil does not enter in. Where our Mother is present, turmoil does not prevail, fear does not conquer. Which of us does not need this, which of us is not sometimes distressed or anxious? How often our heart is a stormy sea, where the waves of our problems pile up and the winds of our troubles do not stop blowing! Mary is our secure ark in the midst of the flood. It will not be ideas or technology that will give us comfort or hope, but our Mother's face, her hands that caress our life, her mantle that gives us shelter. Let us learn how to find refuge, going each day to our Mother.

Reflection

Mary's mantle is another image for her womb. We are invited to stay under the mantle of Mary, in the womb of Mary. "Where our Mother is at home, the devil does not enter in … fear does not conquer": our Mother is always "at home" when we are in her womb. She wants us to find refuge there not only once or a few times each day, but as constantly as a baby finds refuge in its mother's womb.

Remember the last time you were distressed. Give it to Our Lady in her womb. Remember the things that make you anxious and place them in our Mother's womb. As you give up your stresses to Mary, let your anxious parts feel her firm support, secure refuge, tender caresses, and absolute safety from any spiritual harm.

Prayers

Sub Tuum Praesidium
Litany of the Holy Spirit or Veni Sancte Spiritus
Rosary (or at least one decade), followed by the
    Litany of Loreto
Prayer of Entrustment to the Womb of Mary

Week of Knowledge of Jesus Christ

❖

.

Introduction

❖

The culmination of Marian consecration according to the model of St. Louis de Montfort is really consecration to Jesus Christ. For this reason, our journey of preparation concludes with a week focused on Jesus Christ. He is, after all, the Alpha and the Omega, the beginning and the end. He is our Savior and Lord.

St. Louis de Montfort intuited that a sweet and easy path to total consecration to Jesus Christ would be through Mary. As we have learned, this consecration happens particularly through the womb of Mary. That is where the God-Man was formed, and so that is where the "man-gods" can be formed. Jesus Christ is God by nature, but He makes us sharers in His divinity, that is, "God" by grace. This process of divinization is gradual, and the mold is the womb of Mary. So we enter into the womb of Mary not simply out of love for Mary but in order to be transformed into Christ her Son.

As we discussed earlier, however, the concupiscence of Original Sin fundamentally drives us to become god without God. We seek control and self-sufficiency. We want to depend on God only until we arrive at a point when we think we no longer need to depend on Him. We do the same with other people: we are resistant to enter into truly interdependent relationships that are committed and eternal. Because of the wounds of broken trust, we tend to keep escape routes open in case things do not work out. But total consecration to Jesus Christ is a decision to close the escape routes in our relationship with God. It involves our whole mind, heart, body, and soul. It promises our devotion to Christ not only in this moment but in all the moments in the future as well: in time and in eternity.

We make this total consecration through Mary. As we place ourselves in her womb, we let ourselves develop the qualities of Jesus Christ, her Son. We need to develop especially the countercultural qualities that reverse the pattern of Original Sin: the qualities of trust and dependency on God. We develop this trust through prayer and through interdependent relationships with others. Interdependence is part of the life of Jesus. He placed His life in the hands of others, starting with Mary and Joseph and extending to His apostles and disciples. He placed His life so radically in the hands of others that He gave them the power to take His life away—but He never took His trust and love away.

In this Week of Knowledge of Jesus Christ, we focus on the way that Jesus became poor, little, weak, and dependent. We focus on His powerlessness and His dependency on others in His earthly life, and we focus on His ongoing powerlessness in the Eucharist and the dependency and trust that He still gives to us in our response to His Eucharistic Presence. We also focus on the illumination He brings us in the Resurrection and the way He made Himself subject to death. After each day's meditation, we will pray a Litany of the Powerlessness of Jesus, focusing on the way that Jesus, who always had the power of God, truly emptied Himself and subjected Himself to our human limitations, becoming powerless like us. We pray that we might lovingly embrace the powerlessness that He embraced and find all our power in our trust in God. We will pray also a Litany of Jesus Christ Living in the Womb of Mary, asking God to deepen our understanding of how He "consecrated" Himself to Mary in her womb. Thirdly, we will use a prayer written by St. Thomas Aquinas to meditate on the humility of Jesus in His Eucharistic Presence; we strongly encourage you to attend Mass each day this week and offer this prayer before Holy Communion. Lastly, we will continue our Prayer of Entrustment to the Womb of Mary.

Let us ask the Holy Spirit to open our hearts and minds as we begin this week of knowledge of Jesus Christ.

Jesus Is Little, Near, and Real

Reading 1 *Isaiah 66:1–2*

Thus says the Lord:
Heaven is my throne
and the earth is my footstool;
what is the house which you would build for me,
and what is the place of my rest?
All these things my hand has made,
and so all these things are mine,
says the Lord.
But this is the man to whom I will look,
he that is humble and contrite in spirit,
and trembles at my word.

Reading 2 *Pope Francis's homily for Mass on the Occasion of the 1050th Anniversary of the Baptism of Poland near the Shrine of Częstochowa, July 28, 2016*

God saves us, then, by making Himself *little*, *near*, and *real*. First God makes Himself *little*. The Lord, who is "meek and humble of heart" (Matt. 11:29), especially loves the little ones, to whom the kingdom of God is revealed (Matt. 11:25); they are great in His eyes and He looks to them (cf. Isa. 66:2). He especially loves them because they are opposed to the "pride of life" that belongs to the world (cf. 1 John 2:16). The little ones speak His own language, that of the humble love that brings freedom. So He calls the simple and receptive to be His spokespersons; He entrusts to them the revelation of His name and the secrets of His heart. Our minds turn to so many sons and daughters of your own people, like the martyrs [who] made the defenseless power of the Gospel shine forth, like those ordinary yet remarkable people who bore witness to the Lord's love amid great trials, and those meek and powerful heralds of mercy who were St. John Paul II and St. Faustina. Through these "channels" of His love, the Lord has granted priceless gifts to the whole Church and to all mankind. It is significant that this anniversary of the Baptism of your people exactly coincides with the Jubilee of mercy.

Then, too, God is *near*, His kingdom is at hand (cf. Mark 1:15). The Lord does not want to be feared like a powerful and aloof sovereign. He does not want to remain on His throne in Heaven or in history books, but loves to come down to our everyday affairs, to walk with us. As we think of the gift of a millennium so filled with faith, we do well before all else to thank God for having walked with your people, having taken you by the hand, as a father takes the hand of his child, and accompanied you in so many situations. That is what we, too, in the Church, are constantly called to do: to listen, to get involved and be neighbors, sharing in people's joys and struggles, so that the Gospel can spread ever more consistently and fruitfully: radiating goodness through the transparency of our lives.

Finally, *God is real*. Today's readings make it clear that everything about God's way of acting is real and concrete. Divine wisdom "is like a master worker" and "plays" (cf. Prov. 8:30). The Word becomes flesh, is born of a mother, is born under the

law (cf. Gal. 4:4), has friends, and goes to a party. The eternal is communicated by spending time with people and in concrete situations. Your own history, shaped by the Gospel, the Cross, and fidelity to the Church, has seen the contagious power of a genuine faith, passed down from family to family, from fathers to sons, and above all from mothers and grandmothers, whom we need so much to thank. In particular, you have been able to touch with your hand the real and provident tenderness of the Mother of all, whom I have come here as a pilgrim to venerate and whom we have acclaimed in the Psalm as the "great pride of our nation" (Jth. 15:9).

Reflection

"The little ones speak His own language." We can imagine how twin babies communicate in such a simple way in the womb or how a baby in the womb communicates so simply with his mother. The language of love is always simple: gestures of tenderness, embraces, a mother feeding her baby with her body, a mother holding her baby in her arms. This is the first language that Jesus spoke—a language of touch, of food, of kisses and embraces. And it is the last language that He and we speak in our last moments of life.

If we let ourselves be little like Jesus, we can then feel the nearness of Jesus, who draws close to our weakness to bring the tender touch of the Father, as well as the realness of Jesus, who does not settle for ideas but turns them into gestures of love. We therefore must allow ourselves to be little, enfolded in the love of Mary's womb.

Prayers

Litany of the Powerlessness of Jesus
Litany of Jesus Christ Living in the Womb of Mary
Prayer before Holy Communion
Prayer of Entrustment to the Womb of Mary

Christ Became Poor

Reading 1 *2 Corinthians 8:9*

For you know the grace of our Lord Jesus Christ, that though he was rich, yet for your sake he became poor, so that by his poverty you might become rich.

Reading 2 *Pope Francis's Message for Lent 2014,*
December 26, 2013

[Christ] does not reveal Himself cloaked in worldly power and wealth but rather in weakness and poverty: "though He was rich, yet for your sake He became poor." Christ, the eternal Son of God, one with the Father in power and glory, chose to be poor; He came amongst us and drew near to each of us; He set aside His glory and emptied Himself so that He could be like us in all things (cf. Phil. 2:7; Heb. 4:15). God's becoming man is a great mystery! But the reason for all this is His love, a love which is grace, generosity, a desire to draw near, a love which does not hesitate to offer itself in sacrifice for the beloved. Charity, love, is sharing with the one we love in all things. Love makes us similar, it creates equality, it breaks down walls and eliminates distances. God did this with us. Indeed, Jesus "worked with human hands, thought with a human mind, acted by human

choice, and loved with a human heart. Born of the Virgin Mary, He truly became one of us, like us in all things except sin" (*Gaudium et Spes* no. 22).

By making Himself poor, Jesus did not seek poverty for its own sake but, as St. Paul says, "*that by His poverty you might become rich.*" This is no mere play on words or a catch phrase. Rather, it sums up God's logic, the logic of love, the logic of the Incarnation and the Cross. God did not let our salvation drop down from Heaven, like someone who gives alms from their abundance out of a sense of altruism and piety. Christ's love is different! When Jesus stepped into the waters of the Jordan and was baptized by John the Baptist, He did so not because He was in need of repentance or conversion; He did it to be among people who need forgiveness, among us sinners, and to take upon Himself the burden of our sins. In this way He chose to comfort us, to save us, to free us from our misery. It is striking that the Apostle states that we were set free not by Christ's riches but *by His poverty.* Yet St. Paul is well aware of the "the unsearchable riches of Christ" (Eph. 3:8), that He is "heir of all things" (Heb. 1:2).

So what is this poverty by which Christ frees us and enriches us? It is His way of loving us, His way of being our neighbor, just as the Good Samaritan was neighbor to the man left half dead by the side of the road (cf. Luke 10:25ff). What gives us true freedom, true salvation, and true happiness is the compassion, tenderness, and solidarity of His love. Christ's poverty which enriches us is His taking flesh and bearing our weaknesses and sins as an expression of God's infinite mercy to us. Christ's poverty is the greatest treasure of all: Jesus' wealth is that of His boundless confidence in God the Father, His constant trust, His desire always and only to do the Father's will and give glory to Him. Jesus is rich in the same way as a child who feels loved and who loves its parents, without doubting their love and tenderness for an instant. Jesus' wealth lies in His being *the Son*; His unique relationship with the Father is the sovereign prerogative of this Messiah who is poor. When Jesus asks us to take up His "yoke which is easy," He asks us to be enriched by His "poverty which is rich" and His "richness which is poor," to share His filial and fraternal Spirit, to become sons and daughters in the Son, brothers and sisters in the firstborn Brother (cf. Rom. 8:29).

It has been said that the only real regret lies in not being a saint (L. Bloy); we could also say that there is only one real kind of poverty: not living as children of God and brothers and sisters of Christ.

Reflection

Jesus came to share His wealth with us. Pope Francis explains the wealth of Jesus: "Jesus' wealth is that of His boundless confidence in God the Father, His constant trust"; and he further clarifies: "Jesus' wealth lies in His being *the Son*; His unique relationship with the Father."

To share this wealth with us, Jesus became poor. He accepted human love—the love of Joseph and Mary—in place of divine love. He accepted human parents in place of His divine Father, and human helplessness in place of His divine power. But because Jesus could not be separated from His divine Father or from His Father's divine power, He actually filled the poverty of human love with divine love. Now we, too, who are poor, can experience the wealth of Christ. Because we can call His Father "our Father," we can learn about His Fatherhood from our human fathers and mothers, and we can receive glimpses of divine love through our experiences of impoverished, human love.

Our human experience has been radically transformed because Jesus has entered fully into it and blessed all of it as the way to receive His wealth: His boundless confidence in the

Father and the richness of the Father's love. "Jesus is rich in the same way as a child who feels loved and who loves its parents, without doubting their love and tenderness for an instant." And so, by being conceived in Mary's womb so we might share His experience, Jesus has made a way for us to share in that richness.

So let us ask ourselves whether we embrace the poverty and powerlessness that unites us to Jesus in Mary's womb, or whether we are in danger of having the regret of not becoming a saint. Let us practice praying the Our Father from a place of humility and open our hearts to receive the Father's love through the impoverished human loves in our lives.

Prayers

Litany of the Powerlessness of Jesus
Litany of Jesus Christ Living in the Womb of Mary
Prayer before Holy Communion
Prayer of Entrustment to the Womb of Mary

The Humility of Jesus in the Eucharist

Reading 1

John 6:55–67

"For my flesh is food indeed, and my blood is drink indeed. He who eats my flesh and drinks my blood abides in me, and I in him. As the living Father sent me, and I live because of the Father, so he who eats me will live because of me. This is the bread which came down from heaven, not such as the fathers ate and died; he who eats this bread will live forever." This he said in the synagogue, as he taught at Capernaum.

Many of his disciples, when they heard it, said, "This is a hard saying; who can listen to it?" But Jesus, knowing in himself that his disciples murmured at it, said to them, "Do you take offense at this? Then what if you were to see the Son of man ascending where he was before? It is the spirit that gives life, the flesh is of no avail; the words that I have spoken to you are spirit and life. But there are some of you that do not believe." For Jesus knew from the first who those were that did not believe, and who it was that should betray him. And he said, "This is why I told you that no one can come to me unless it is granted him by the Father."

After this many of his disciples drew back and no longer went about with him. Jesus said to the Twelve, "Will you also go away?"

Reading 2

Let us learn from the saints who have written and spoken about the humility of Jesus in the Eucharist:

From St. Francis of Assisi's *Letter to the Entire Order (1225–1226)*:

Listen, my brothers: If the Blessed Virgin is so honored, as is becoming, because she carried Him in her most holy womb;

if the Baptist trembled and did not dare to touch the holy head of God; if the tomb in which He lay for some time is held in veneration, how holy, just, and fitting must be he who touches with his hands, receives in his heart and mouth, and offers to others to be received the One who is not about to die but who is to conquer and be glorified, upon whom the angels longed to gaze....

Let everyone be struck with fear, let the whole world tremble, and let the heavens exult when Christ, the Son of the living God, is present on the altar in the hands of a priest! O wonderful loftiness and stupendous dignity! O sublime humility! O humble sublimity! The Lord of the universe, God and the Son of God, so humbles Himself under an ordinary piece of bread! Brothers, look at the humility of God, and pour out your hearts before Him! Humble yourselves, that you may be exalted by Him! Hold back nothing of yourselves for yourselves, that He who gives Himself totally to you may receive you totally![6]

From the *Diary of St. Faustina* (entry 80):

O Jesus, Divine Prisoner of Love, when I consider Your love and how You emptied Yourself for me, my senses fail me. You hide Your inconceivable majesty and lower Yourself to miserable me. O King of Glory, though You hide Your beauty, yet the eye of my soul rends the veil. I see the angelic choirs giving You honor without cease, and all the heavenly Powers praising You without cease, and without cease they are saying: Holy, Holy, Holy.

Oh, who will comprehend Your love and Your unfathomable mercy toward us! O Prisoner of Love, I lock up my poor

---

[6] Regis J. Armstrong, J. A. Wayne Hellmann, William J. Short, eds., *Francis of Assisi: Early Documents*, vol. 1, *The Saint* (New York: New City Press, 1999), 118.

heart in this tabernacle, that it may adore You without cease night and day. I know of no obstacle in this adoration, and even though I be physically distant, my heart is always with You. Nothing can put a stop to my love for You. No obstacles exist for me. O my Jesus, I will console You for all the ingratitude, the blasphemies, the coldness, the hatred of the wicked, the sacrileges. O Jesus, I want to burn as a pure offering and to be consumed before the throne of Your hiddenness. I plead with You unceasingly for poor dying sinners.[7]

From St. Teresa of Calcutta:

Like her [Mary], let us be full of zeal to go in haste to give Jesus to others. She was full of grace when, at the Annunciation, she received Jesus. Like her, we too become full of grace every time we receive Holy Communion. It is the same Jesus whom she received and whom we receive at Mass. As soon as she received Him, she went with haste to give Him to John. For us also, as soon as we receive Jesus in Holy Communion, let us go in haste to give Him to our Sisters, to our poor, to the sick, to the dying, to the lepers, to the unwanted, the unloved, etc. By this we make Jesus present in the world of today.[8]

From St. Thérèse of Lisieux on the Communion of Midnight Mass:

God would have to work a little miracle to make me grow up in an instant, and this miracle He performed on that unforgettable Christmas day. On that luminous night which sheds such

[7] Saint Maria Faustina Kowalska, Diary: Divine Mercy in My Soul (Stockbridge, MA: Marian Press, 2020), 41.
[8] Mother Teresa, Where There Is Love, There Is God, ed. Brian Kolodiejchyk (New York: Doubleday, 2010), 340.

light on the delights of the Holy Trinity, Jesus, the gentle, little Child of only one hour, changed the night of my soul into rays of light. On that night when He made Himself subject to weakness and suffering for love of me, He made me strong and courageous, arming me with His weapons. Since that night I have never been defeated in any combat, but rather walked from victory to victory, beginning, so to speak, "to run as a giant"!⁹

Reflection

Do we see the humility of Jesus, who continually comes to us in a way that makes us easily overlook Him? We cannot by our human senses tell the difference between a consecrated host and an unconsecrated host—we cannot see, taste, or smell the difference between Jesus and a simple piece of bread! Yet Jesus humbles Himself at each Mass and comes to us in the mundane substances of bread and wine.

How do we, on the other hand, promote ourselves? Are we offended when others do not know who we are? Do we push ourselves forward to make sure we are seen, or correct others when they do not acknowledge our credentials? Do we feel self-important?

Consider how contrary these attitudes are to the humility of Jesus, who remains anonymously, invisibly hidden beneath the appearance of bread and wine and then is hidden away in a tabernacle. Yet isn't this humility, this hiddenness so like a baby in the womb, especially when that baby is so small that the mother does not even appear to be, or perhaps even know that she is, pregnant? Are we willing to be so small, so hidden, so overlooked as to be a tiny, tiny baby in the womb of Mary?

---

⁹ St. Thérèse of Lisieux, *Story of a Soul*, trans. John Clarke (Washington, D.C.: ICS Publications, 2005), 153.

If so, then we are drawing closer to fulfilling the command of Jesus: "Learn from me; for I am gentle and lowly in heart" (Matt. 11:29).

Prayers

We pray first with Mother Teresa: "Mary, Mother of Jesus, give us your heart, so beautiful, so pure, so immaculate, so full of love and humility, that we may be able to receive Jesus in the Bread of Life, love Him as you love Him, and serve Him in the distressing disguise of the poor."

Litany of the Powerlessness of Jesus
Litany of Jesus Christ Living in the Womb of Mary
Prayer before Holy Communion
Prayer of Entrustment to the Womb of Mary

Mary, the Eucharist, and the Incarnation

Reading 1 *Luke 1:34–35*

And Mary said to the angel, "How can this be, since I have no husband?" And the angel said to her, "The Holy Spirit will come upon you, and the power of the Most High will overshadow you; therefore the child to be born will be called holy, the Son of God."

Reading 2 *Luke 22:19–20*

And he took bread, and when he had given thanks he broke it and gave it to them, saying, "This is my body which is given for you. Do this in remembrance of me." And likewise the chalice after supper, saying, "This cup which is poured out for you is the new covenant in my blood."

Reading 3 *Pope St. John Paul II's encyclical letter
Ecclesia de Eucharistia
(April 17, 2003), nos. 55–56*

In a certain sense, Mary lived her Eucharistic faith even before the institution of the Eucharist, by the very fact that she offered her virginal womb for the Incarnation of God's Word. The Eucharist, while commemorating the Passion and Resurrection, is also in continuity with the Incarnation. At the Annunciation, Mary conceived the Son of God in the physical reality of His Body and Blood, thus anticipating within herself what to some degree happens sacramentally in every believer who receives, under the signs of bread and wine, the Lord's Body and Blood.

As a result, there is a profound analogy between the fiat which Mary said in reply to the angel and the amen which every believer says when receiving the Body of the Lord. Mary was asked to believe that the One whom she conceived "through the Holy Spirit" was "the Son of God" (Luke 1:30–35). In continuity with the Virgin's faith, in the Eucharistic mystery we are asked to believe that the same Jesus Christ, Son of God and Son of Mary, becomes present in His full humanity and divinity under the signs of bread and wine.

"Blessed is she who believed" (Luke 1:45). Mary also anticipated, in the mystery of the Incarnation, the Church's Eucharistic faith. When, at the Visitation, she bore in her womb the Word made flesh, she became in some way a "tabernacle"—the first "tabernacle" in history—in which the Son of God, still invisible to our human gaze, allowed Himself to be adored by Elizabeth, radiating His light as it were through the eyes and the voice of Mary. And is not the enraptured gaze of Mary as she contemplated the face of the newborn Christ and cradled Him in her arms that unparalleled model of love which should inspire us every time we receive Eucharistic communion?...

What must Mary have felt as she heard from the mouth of Peter, John, James, and the other Apostles the words spoken at the Last Supper: "This is my body which is given for you" (Luke 22:19)? The Body given up for us and made present under sacramental signs was the same Body which she had conceived in her womb! For Mary, receiving the Eucharist must have somehow

meant welcoming once more into her womb that heart which had beat in unison with hers and reliving what she had experienced at the foot of the Cross.

Reflection

Every Mass brings us to the womb of Mary, the first tabernacle where Christ first became present in His Body and Blood. Christ spent the first nine months of His life in the womb of Mary, and therefore, every tabernacle is a copy of that first tabernacle. If we want to be close to Jesus in His Body and Blood, to hide ourselves away in the tabernacle with Him, we must consecrate ourselves to Mary, hiding ourselves away in her womb. Jesus remains there in all His hiddenness and littleness, in that first tabernacle.

Are we too big to fit, too full of ourselves, too busy with the things of the world? Or can we let ourselves be hidden in love to find the Hidden Love who remains wrapped in love? Can we allow ourselves to be confined to God's will as we dwell in the womb of Mary? Can we join our lives to the heart of Mary, who was always freely confined to God's will?

Mary teaches us to make a home, a tabernacle, a womb in our hearts for Jesus to remain always. We make this home by uttering with her our Yes to God's will: fiat.

Prayers

Litany of the Powerlessness of Jesus
Litany of Jesus Christ Living in the Womb of Mary
Prayer before Holy Communion
Prayer of Entrustment to the Womb of Mary

God Seeks Man in the Womb of Mary

Reading 1 *Luke 15:1–7*

Now the tax collectors and sinners were all drawing near to hear him. And the Pharisees and the scribes murmured, saying, "This man receives sinners and eats with them." So he told them this parable: "What man of you, having a hundred sheep, if he has lost one of them, does not leave the ninety-nine in the wilderness, and go after the one which is lost, until he finds it? And when he has found it, he lays it on his shoulders, rejoicing. And when he comes home, he calls together his friends and his neighbors, saying to them, 'Rejoice with me, for I have found my sheep which was lost.' Just so, I tell you, there will be more joy in heaven over one sinner who repents than over ninety-nine righteous persons who need no repentance."

Reading 2 *Pope St. John Paul II's apostolic letter* Tertio millennio adveniente *(November 10, 1994), no. 7*

In Jesus Christ God not only speaks to man but also seeks him out. The Incarnation of the Son of God attests that God goes in

search of man. Jesus speaks of this search as the finding of a lost sheep (cf. Luke 15:1–7). It is a search which begins in the heart of God and culminates in the Incarnation of the Word. If God goes in search of man, created in His own image and likeness, He does so because He loves him eternally in the Word and wishes to raise him in Christ to the dignity of an adoptive son. God therefore goes in search of man who is His special possession in a way unlike any other creature. Man is God's possession by virtue of a choice made in love: God seeks man out, moved by His fatherly heart.

Why does God seek man out? Because man has turned away from Him, hiding himself as Adam did among the trees of the Garden of Eden (cf. Gen. 3:8–10). Man allowed himself to be led astray by the enemy of God (cf. Gen. 3:13). Satan deceived man, persuading him that he too was a god, that he, like God, was capable of knowing good and evil, ruling the world according to his own will without having to take into account the divine will (cf. Gen. 3:5). Going in search of man through His Son, God wishes to persuade man to abandon the paths of evil which lead him farther and farther afield. "Making him abandon" those paths means making man understand that he is taking the wrong path; it means overcoming the evil which is everywhere found in human history. Overcoming evil: this is the meaning of the Redemption. This is brought about in the sacrifice of Christ, by which man redeems the debt of sin and is reconciled to God. The Son of God became man, taking a body and soul in the womb of the Virgin, precisely for this reason: to become the perfect redeeming sacrifice. The religion of the Incarnation is the religion of the world's Redemption through the sacrifice of Christ, wherein lies victory over evil, over sin, and over death itself. Accepting death on the Cross, Christ at the same time reveals and gives life, because He rises again, and death no longer has power over Him.

Reflection

God is seeking us! He is looking for you. He wants to bring you home. He longs for us, thirsts for us. Where does He go looking? Where we are most helpless, most powerless, most weak, hurting, lost, forgotten, abandoned, overlooked, and hidden. When we are feeling so small that we could fit into a womb, because we are so ashamed that we shrivel up and hide in our sinfulness, because we are so belittled by the harshness and domination of others, or because we feel so weak and insignificant, Christ is seeking us. He becomes small like us. He takes on our sins, the rebukes of the powerful, and the weakness of our humanity. He seeks us in the womb of Mary, embracing all the littleness and pain of being human so that He might fill it with all the sweetness of divine love.

Will you let Him find you? When God called out to Adam, Adam responded to the call. Will you respond when God calls your name, looking for you in your hiding places? Will you let God into your hiding places? We say Yes to these questions when we choose the womb of Mary to be our hiding place, when that is the place we go when we feel little, embarrassed, afraid and lost. Let us practice this today by bringing our places of shame and helplessness into the womb of Mary, where God will always find us.

Prayers

Litany of the Powerlessness of Jesus
Litany of Jesus Christ Living in the Womb of Mary
Prayer before Holy Communion
Prayer of Entrustment to the Womb of Mary

Christ Brings Us Life and Light in Baptism

Reading 1 *Matthew 28:1–10*

Now after the sabbath, toward the dawn of the first day of the week, Mary Magdalene and the other Mary went to see the sepulchre. And behold, there was a great earthquake; for an angel of the Lord descended from heaven and came and rolled back the stone, and sat upon it. His appearance was like lightning, and his raiment white as snow. And for fear of him the guards trembled and became like dead men. But the angel said to the women, "Do not be afraid; for I know that you seek Jesus who was crucified. He is not here; for he has risen, as he said. Come, see the place where he lay. Then go quickly and tell his disciples that he has risen from the dead, and behold, he is going before you to Galilee; there you will see him. Lo, I have told you." So they departed quickly from the tomb with fear and great joy, and ran to tell his disciples. And behold, Jesus met them and said, "Hail!" And they came up and took hold of his feet and worshiped him. Then Jesus said to them, "Do not be afraid; go and tell my brethren to go to Galilee, and there they will see me."

Reading 2

*Pope Benedict XVI's homily
for the Easter Vigil, April 15, 2006*

His death was an act of love. At the Last Supper, He anticipated death and transformed it into self-giving. His existential communion with God was concretely an existential communion with God's love, and this love is the real power against death, it is stronger than death. The Resurrection was like an explosion of light, an explosion of love which dissolved the hitherto indissoluble compenetration of "dying and becoming." It ushered in a new dimension of being, a new dimension of life in which, in a transformed way, matter too was integrated and through which a new world emerges....

The great explosion of the Resurrection has seized us in Baptism so as to draw us on. Thus we are associated with a new dimension of life into which, amid the tribulations of our day, we are already in some way introduced. To live one's own life as a continual entry into this open space: this is the meaning of being baptized, of being Christian. This is the joy of the Easter Vigil. The Resurrection is not a thing of the past, the Resurrection has reached us and seized us. We grasp hold of it, we grasp hold of the risen Lord, and we know that He holds us firmly even when our hands grow weak. We grasp hold of His hand, and thus we also hold on to one another's hands, and we become one single subject, not just one thing. I, but no longer I: this is the formula of Christian life rooted in Baptism, the formula of the Resurrection within time. I, but no longer I: if we live in this way, we transform the world. It is a formula contrary to all ideologies of violence, it is a program opposed to corruption and to the desire for power and possession.

Reading 3

*Pope Benedict XVI's homily
for the Easter Vigil, March 22, 2008*

Through His radical love for us, in which the heart of God and the heart of man touched, Jesus Christ truly took light from

Heaven and brought it to the earth—the light of truth and the fire of love that transform man's being. He brought the light, and now we know who God is and what God is like. Thus we also know what our human situation is: what we are, and for what purpose we exist. When we are baptized, the fire of this light is brought down deep within ourselves. Thus, in the early Church, Baptism was also called the Sacrament of Illumination: God's light enters into us; thus we ourselves become children of light. We must not allow this light of truth, that shows us the path, to be extinguished. We must protect it from all the forces that seek to eliminate it so as to cast us back into darkness regarding God and ourselves. Darkness, at times, can seem comfortable. I can hide and spend my life asleep. Yet we are not called to darkness but to light. In our baptismal promises, we rekindle this light, so to speak, year by year. Yes, I believe that the world and my life are not the product of chance but of eternal Reason and eternal Love, they are created by Almighty God. Yes, I believe that in Jesus Christ, in His Incarnation, in His Cross and Resurrection, the face of God has been revealed; that in Him, God is present in our midst, He unites us and leads us towards our goal, towards eternal Love. Yes, I believe that the Holy Spirit gives us the word of truth and enlightens our hearts; I believe that in the communion of the Church we all become one Body with the Lord, and thus we encounter His Resurrection and eternal life. The Lord has granted us the light of truth. This light is also fire, a powerful force coming from God, a force that does not destroy but seeks to transform our hearts, so that we truly become men of God, and so that His peace can become active in this world.

Reflection

Christ's Resurrection changed everything. He has taken our hands, and He has illumined the way to eternal life. He helps us navigate the treacherous paths of life, picking us up and walking with us—even across the threshold of death. Through His Resurrection, we are reborn, and we live our new lives in Him through Baptism.

Because Jesus has changed us into Himself through Baptism, we are never alone, "we grasp hold of the risen Lord, and we know that He holds us firmly even when our hands grow weak." We do not need to fear our weakness, as He gives us His strength. When we are most desperate, He comes to us and takes us by the hand. When the night is darkest, He brings us the light of Heaven.

"Now we know who God is and what God is like." Now we have the Holy Spirit, the fire from Heaven that warms us and transforms our hearts; the fire that first burned in the heart of Mary, the first redeemed; the fire that warmed the Infant God in her womb and warms each us of us who choose to rest in her womb, beneath her Immaculate Heart.

From the perspective of the womb, this is a matter of looking forward to birth. Whatever difficulties we face, God will bring us through them and help us come to birth to a new life in the Risen Lord. Will you let the light of Heaven shine into the darkest places in your life? Will you take the Hand of the Risen Lord who reaches down to lift you up? Let us look forward to our birth to our eternal life.

Prayers

Litany of the Powerlessness of Jesus
Litany of Jesus Christ Living in the Womb of Mary
Prayer before Holy Communion
Prayer of Entrustment to the Womb of Mary

Jesus Dies, the Word Is Silenced

Reading 1   *Matthew 27:57–61*

When it was evening, there came a rich man from Arimathea, named Joseph, who also was a disciple of Jesus. He went to Pilate and asked for the body of Jesus. Then Pilate ordered it to be given to him. And Joseph took the body, and wrapped it in a clean linen shroud, and laid it in his own new tomb, which he had hewn in the rock; and he rolled a great stone to the door of the tomb, and departed. Mary Magdalene and the other Mary were there, sitting opposite the sepulchre.

Reading 2   *Pope St. John Paul II's Address*
                              in Turin, May 24, 1998, nos. 6–7

The Shroud is also an image of powerlessness: the powerlessness of death, in which the ultimate consequence of the mystery of the Incarnation is revealed. The burial cloth spurs us to measure ourselves against the most troubling aspect of the mystery of the Incarnation, which is also the one that shows with how much truth God truly became man, taking on our condition in all things, except sin. Everyone is shaken by the thought that not

even the Son of God withstood the power of death, but we are all moved at the thought that He so shared our human condition as willingly to subject Himself to the total powerlessness of the moment when life is spent. It is the experience of Holy Saturday, an important stage on Jesus' path to Glory, from which a ray of light shines on the sorrow and death of every person. By reminding us of Christ's victory, faith gives us the certainty that the grave is not the ultimate goal of existence. God calls us to resurrection and immortal life.

The Shroud is an image of silence. There is a tragic silence of incommunicability, which finds its greatest expression in death, and there is the silence of fruitfulness, which belongs to whoever refrains from being heard outwardly in order to delve to the roots of truth and life. The Shroud expresses not only the silence of death but also the courageous and fruitful silence of triumph over the transitory, through total immersion in God's eternal present. It thus offers a moving confirmation of the fact that the merciful omnipotence of our God is not restrained by any power of evil but knows instead how to make the very power of evil contribute to good. Our age needs to rediscover the fruitfulness of silence in order to overcome the dissipation of sounds, images, and chatter that too often prevent the voice of God from being heard.

Reflection

Jesus never fled from the limitations of our humanity. Like all of us, Jesus ended as He began: helpless, powerless, and silent. But His acceptance of our humanity gives us victory. From His first moment in Mary's womb to His last breath on the Cross, Jesus drank the full cup of our humanity all the way to the dregs. As St. John Paul II reminds us, this knowledge should comfort us. We are never alone when we experience our human weakness and powerlessness. We are never abandoned by the One who has shared our humanity with us and who will carry us through.

We should also remember that Jesus was accompanied in His weakest moments by Mary His Mother: she was by His side during His infancy, His childhood, His Passion, and His death. And so He gives her to us to accompany us throughout our lives. When we feel most weak and poor, we must remember that we are safely enclosed in the womb of Mary, who always loves us and cares for us.

Will you let Mary accompany you today in your weakness and suffering? Will you let Mary support you in your greatest difficulties? Will you let Mary help you to say Yes, like Jesus did, to drinking the full cup of your humanity?

Prayers

Litany of the Powerlessness of Jesus
Litany of Jesus Christ Living in the Womb of Mary
Prayer before Holy Communion
Prayer of Entrustment to the Womb of Mary

Total Consecration to Jesus through Mary

❖

Making Our Total Consecration to Jesus through Mary

After thirty-three days of preparation, we are ready to make, or renew, our consecration to Jesus through Mary.[10] We encourage all to partake in the sacraments of Penance and Reconciliation and Holy Communion as soon as possible as a final step of preparation for the consecration: there is no better preparation than a humble and sincere sacramental Confession and a devout participation in the Holy Eucharist including sacramental Communion. If it is not possible, for some reason, to receive the sacraments, however, at least make

---

[10] St. Louis de Montfort outlined concisely several recommendations for how to live this day in his book *True Devotion to Mary*. An online copy of this book can be found at https://www.ecatholic2000. com/montfort/true/devotion.shtml.

a sincere act of contrition and a spiritual Communion before making your consecration.

While St. Louis de Montfort's original text for the consecration can be found in the first appendix at the end of this book,[11] we also have provided a slightly altered version of his Total Consecration to Jesus through Mary that captures all the depth and theological importance yet adjusts the language slightly to favor the loving image of being in the womb as opposed to the image of slavery. As expressed in the Introduction at the beginning of our journey, there is no greater "slavery" than being in the womb, but being in the womb carries none of the negative connotations that are found with "slavery," especially in light of American history.

One other adjustment in the prayer of Total Consecration is more corrective. Though it was certainly well-intended by St. Louis de Montfort, the notion that Jesus would reject or despise us, and the idea that Mary is somehow a better mediator or a more merciful advocate than her Son, is contrary to Catholic teaching. St. Louis de Montfort likely expressed his prayer in this way according to the cultural idioms of his time and to inspire greater trust in Our Lady, but his expression is in danger of reinforcing false images of Jesus that could undermine our absolute trust in His Infinite Mercy. And so we have adjusted that sentence of St. Louis de Montfort's formula. We leave it to our readers to decide which formula for Consecration they would prefer, but we offer ours especially for the sensitive souls who need more comfort and trust than harshness and fear.

Whichever version of the prayer you choose, we recommend that you write out the consecration for the sake of investing

---

[11] You may also use a more modern translation of his text, such as the one found at http://www.montfortian.info/ttj/1.-act-of-consecration.html.

more love and attention in the words and in order to solemnize this important moment of prayer. Typing out the prayer with a word processor, printing a copy, and signing it is also appropriate.

Act of Total Consecration to Jesus through Mary

Eternal and incarnate Wisdom, most lovable and adorable Jesus, true God and true man, only Son of the eternal Father and of Mary always Virgin, I profoundly adore You, who dwell in the splendor of Your Father from all eternity and were incarnate in the virginal womb of Mary, Your most worthy Mother.

I thank You for having emptied Yourself in assuming the condition of a slave in order to set me free from the cruel slavery of the evil one. I praise and glorify You for having willingly chosen to obey Mary, Your holy Mother, in all things, so that through surrendering all my power and self-determination by dwelling in her womb, I may always be Your faithful lover.

But I must confess that I have not kept the vows and promises that I had made to You so solemnly at my Baptism. I have not fulfilled my obligations, and I do not deserve to be called Your child or even Your loving slave.

Because I have turned away from You in my sins and I feel so little and poor in my weakness, I do not feel great enough to approach Your divine Majesty, but I do feel that I can approach You in Your littleness as You dwell in Mary's womb. That is why I turn to the intercession and the mercy of Your holy Mother, whom You Yourself have given me to be my meeting place with You. Through her, in her womb, I hope to obtain from You contrition and pardon for my sins and that Wisdom whom I desire to dwell in me always.

I turn to you, then, Mary Immaculate, living tabernacle of God, in whom eternal Wisdom willed to receive the adoration of men, women, and angels. I greet you as Queen of Heaven and earth, for all that is under God has been made subject to your sovereignty. I call upon you, the unfailing refuge of sinners, confident in your mercy that has never forsaken anyone. Grant my desire for divine Wisdom and, in support of my petition, accept the promises and the offering of myself, which I now make, conscious of my littleness.

I, _____, an unfaithful sinner, renew and ratify today through you my baptismal promises. I renounce forever Satan, his empty promises, and his evil designs, and I give myself completely to Jesus Christ, the incarnate Wisdom, to carry my cross after Him for the rest of my life and to be more faithful to Him than I have been until now.

This day, with the whole court of Heaven as witness, I choose you, Mary, as my Mother and Queen. I surrender and consecrate myself to you, body and soul, with all that I possess, both spiritual and material, even including the spiritual value of all my actions, past, present, and to come. I give you the full right to dispose of me and all that belongs to me, without any reservations, in whatever way you please, for the greater glory of God in time and throughout eternity. I entrust myself to your loving, maternal care with the same total abandon as the Baby Jesus, who chose to dwell in your womb.

Accept, gracious Virgin, this little offering of myself, to honor and imitate the obedience that eternal Wisdom willingly chose to have toward you, His Mother. I wish to acknowledge the authority that both of you have over this pitiful sinner. By my offering, I wish also to thank God for the privileges bestowed on you by the Blessed Trinity. I solemnly declare that for the future I will try to honor and obey you in all things as an infant in your womb. O admirable Mother, present me to your dear Son as His little twin in your womb, so that He who redeemed me through you will now receive me through you.

Mother of mercy, grant me the favor of obtaining the true Wisdom of God, and so make me one of those whom you love, teach, and guide, whom you nourish and protect as your own infant in your womb.

Virgin most faithful, make me in everything so committed a disciple, imitator, and twin infant of Jesus, your Son, incarnate Wisdom, that I may become, through your intercession and example, fully mature with the fullness that Jesus possessed on earth and with the fullness of His glory in Heaven. Amen.

Appendices

St. Louis de Montfort's Consecration

St. Louis de Montfort's Consecration of Ourselves to Jesus Christ, the Incarnate Wisdom, by the Hands of Mary

O eternal and Incarnate Wisdom! O sweetest and most Adorable Jesus! True God and True Man, only Son of the Eternal Father, and of Mary always Virgin! I adore Thee profoundly in the bosom and splendors of Thy Father during eternity; and I adore Thee also in the Virginal bosom of Mary, Thy most worthy Mother, in the time of Thine Incarnation.

I give Thee thanks for that Thou hast annihilated Thyself, in taking the form of a slave, in order to rescue me from the cruel slavery of the devil. I praise and glorify Thee for that Thou hast been pleased to submit Thyself to Mary, Thy holy Mother, in all things, in order to make me Thy faithful slave through her. But, alas! ungrateful and faithless as I have been, I have not kept the promises which I made so solemnly to Thee in my Baptism; I have not fulfilled my obligations; I do not deserve to be called

Thy son, nor yet Thy slave; and as there is nothing in me which does not merit Thine anger and Thy repulse, I dare no more come by myself before Thy Most Holy and August Majesty. It is on this account that I have recourse to the intercession of Thy most holy Mother, whom Thou hast given me for a mediatrix with Thee. It is by her means that I hope to obtain of Thee contrition, and the pardon of my sins, the acquisition and the preservation of wisdom. I salute thee, then, O immaculate Mary, living tabernacle of the Divinity, where the Eternal Wisdom willed to be hidden and to be adored by Angels and by men. I hail thee, O Queen of Heaven and earth, to whose empire everything is subject which is under God.

I salute thee, O sure refuge of sinners, whose mercy fails to no one. Hear the desires which I have of the Divine Wisdom; and for that end receive the vows and offerings which my lowness presents to thee. I, [Name], a faithless sinner—I renew and ratify today in thy hands the vows of my Baptism; I renounce forever Satan, his pomps, and works; and I give myself entirely to Jesus Christ, the Incarnate Wisdom, to carry my cross after Him all the days of my life, and to be more faithful to Him than I have ever been before.

In the presence of all the heavenly court I choose thee this day for my Mother and Mistress. I deliver and consecrate to thee, as thy slave, my body and soul, my goods, both interior and exterior, and even the value of all my good actions, past, present, and future; leaving to you the entire and full right of disposing of me, and all that belongs to me, without exception, according to thy good pleasure, to the greatest glory of God, in time and in eternity.

Receive, O benignant Virgin, this little offering of my slavery, in the honor of, and in union with, that subjection which the Eternal Wisdom deigned to have to thy Maternity, in homage to the power which both of you have over this little worm and miserable sinner, and in thanksgiving for the privileges with which the Holy Trinity hath favored thee. I protest that I wish henceforth, as thy true slave, to seek thy honor and to obey thee in all things.

O admirable Mother, present me to thy dear Son as His eternal slave, so that as He hath redeemed me by thee, by thee He may receive me. O Mother of mercy, get me the grace to obtain the true Wisdom of God; and for that end put me in the number of those whom thou lovest, whom thou teachest, whom thou conductest, and whom thou nourishest and protectest, as thy children and thy slaves.

O faithful Virgin, make me in all things so perfect a disciple, imitator, and slave of the Incarnate Wisdom, Jesus Christ thy Son, that I may attain, by thy intercession, and by thy example, to the fullness of His age on earth, and of His glory in the heavens. Amen.[12]

---

[12] Louis de Montfort, *True Devotion to Mary*, trans. Frederick William Faber (Robson, Levey, and Franklyn: London, 1863; eCatholic2000.com, 2018), https://www.ecatholic2000.com/montfort/true/devotion.shtml.

Prayers

Ave Maris Stella

Hail, bright star of ocean,
God's own Mother blest,
Ever sinless Virgin,
Gate of heavenly rest.

Taking that sweet Ave
Which from Gabriel came,
Peace confirm within us,
Changing Eva's name.

Break the captives' fetters,
Light on blindness pour,
All our ills expelling,
Every bliss implore.

Show thyself a Mother;
May the Word Divine,
Born for us thy Infant,
Hear our prayers through thine.

Virgin all excelling,
Mildest of the mild,
Freed from guilt, preserve us,
Pure and undefiled.

Keep our life all spotless,
Make our way secure,
Till we find in Jesus,
Joy forevermore.

Through the highest Heaven
To the Almighty Three,
Father, Son, and Spirit,
One same glory be. Amen.

Litany of the Holy Spirit

Lord, have mercy on us, Christ have mercy on us.

Lord, have mercy on us. Father all powerful, have mercy on us.

Jesus, Eternal Son of the Father, Redeemer of the world, *save us.*

Spirit of the Father and the Son, boundless Life of both, *sanctify us.*

Holy Trinity, *hear us.*

Holy Spirit, who proceedest from the Father and the Son, *enter our hearts.*

Holy Spirit, who art equal to the Father and the Son, *enter our hearts.*

Promise of God the Father, *have mercy on us.*

Ray of heavenly light, *have mercy on us.*

Author of all good, *have mercy on us.*

Source of heavenly water, *have mercy on us.*

Consuming Fire, *have mercy on us.*

Ardent Charity, *have mercy on us.*

Spiritual Unction, *have mercy on us.*

Spirit of love and truth, *have mercy on us.*

Spirit of wisdom and understanding, *have mercy on us.*

Spirit of counsel and fortitude, *have mercy on us.*
Spirit of knowledge and piety, *have mercy on us.*
Spirit of the fear of the Lord, *have mercy on us.*
Spirit of grace and prayer, *have mercy on us.*
Spirit of peace and meekness, *have mercy on us.*
Spirit of modesty and innocence, *have mercy on us.*
Holy Spirit, the Comforter, *have mercy on us.*
Holy Spirit, the Sanctifier, *have mercy on us.*
Holy Spirit, who governs the Church, *have mercy on us.*
Gift of God the Most High, *have mercy on us.*
Spirit who fills the universe, *have mercy on us.*
Spirit of the adoption of the children of God,
    have mercy on us.
Holy Spirit, *inspire us with horror of sin.*
Holy Spirit, *come and renew the face of the earth.*
Holy Spirit, *shed Your Light into our souls.*
Holy Spirit, *engrave Your law in our hearts.*
Holy Spirit, *inflame us with the flame of Your love.*
Holy Spirit, *open to us the treasures of Your graces.*
Holy Spirit, *teach us to pray well.*
Holy Spirit, *enlighten us with Your heavenly inspirations.*
Holy Spirit, *lead us in the way of salvation.*
Holy Spirit, *grant us the only necessary knowledge.*
Holy Spirit, *inspire in us the practice of good.*
Holy Spirit, *grant us the merits of all virtues.*
Holy Spirit, *make us persevere in justice.*
Holy Spirit, *be our everlasting reward.*
Lamb of God, You take away the sins of the world,
    send us Your Holy Spirit.
Lamb of God, You take away the sins of the world,
    pour down into our souls the gifts of the Holy Spirit.
Lamb of God, You take away the sins of the world,
    grant us the Spirit of wisdom and piety.

Come, Holy Spirit! Fill the hearts of Your faithful and
   enkindle in them the fire of Your love.

Let us pray: Grant, O merciful Father, that Your Divine
Spirit may enlighten, inflame, and purify us, that He may
penetrate us with His heavenly dew and make us fruitful
in good works, through Our Lord Jesus Christ, Your Son,
who lives and reigns with You in the unity of the same
Spirit, one God, forever and ever. Amen.

Litany of Jesus Christ Living in the Womb of Mary

Jesus Christ, knit so wonderfully in the womb of Mary,
   have mercy on us.
Jesus, conceived by the Holy Spirit in the womb of Mary,
   have mercy on us.
Jesus, uniquely Man from the moment of conception in
   the womb of Mary, *have mercy on us.*
Jesus, through whom the world was made, who was
   formed in the womb of Mary, *have mercy on us.*
Jesus, Word made flesh, who took on a human Body in
   the womb of Mary, *have mercy on us.*
Jesus, revealed by God the Father, yet concealed in the
   womb of Mary, *have mercy on us.*
Jesus, subject to human development in the womb of
   Mary, *have mercy on us.*
Jesus, whose precious Blood first flowed through tiny
   arteries and veins in the womb of Mary,
   have mercy on us.
Jesus, hidden nine months in the womb of Mary,
   have mercy on us.

Jesus, only begotten of the Father, who assumed flesh in the womb of Mary, *have mercy on us.*

Jesus, begotten by God and nourished by the substance and blood of His Most Holy Mother in the womb of Mary, *have mercy on us.*

Jesus, leaping from eternity into time in the womb of Mary, *have mercy on us.*

Jesus, revealing with His Father and the Holy Spirit all wisdom and knowledge to His Most Holy Mother in the womb of Mary, *have mercy on us.*

Jesus, aware of His role as Redeemer in the womb of Mary, *have mercy on us.*

Jesus, Sanctifier of His precursor from the womb of Mary, *have mercy on us.*

Jesus, Eternal Word, Divine Child, embraced by the Father in the womb of Mary, *have mercy on us.*

Jesus, raising His Mother to the heights of sanctification in the womb of Mary, *have mercy on us.*

Jesus, everlasting delight of Heaven in the womb of Mary, *have mercy on us.*

Jesus, manifesting His Incarnation to His Holy Mother in the womb of Mary, *have mercy on us.*

Jesus, adored and contemplated by His Mother in the sanctuary of the womb of Mary, *have mercy on us.*

Jesus, before whom the angels prostrated themselves in the womb of Mary, *have mercy on us.*

Jesus, in whom the very angels beheld the humanity of the Infant God and the union of the two natures of the Word in the virginal womb of Mary, *have mercy on us.*

Jesus, our Protector and Savior, asleep in the inviolable womb of Mary, *have mercy on us.*

Jesus, whose Holy Limbs first budded in the womb of
Mary, *have mercy on us.*
Jesus, whose Sacred Heart first began beating in the
womb of Mary, *have mercy on us.*
Jesus, whose Godhead the world cannot contain, weighing
only a few grams in the womb of Mary, *have mercy on us.*
Jesus, whose Divine Immensity once measured only tenths
of an inch in the womb of Mary, *have mercy on us.*
Jesus, whose Divine Grasp outreaches the universe and
yet was cradled in the womb of Mary, *have mercy on us.*
Jesus, Sacrificial Lamb, docile Infant in the womb of
Mary, *have mercy on us.*
Jesus, who was to suffer the agony and passion of death,
accepting the human capacity for pain and grief, in
the womb of Mary, *have mercy on us.*
Jesus, foretelling His Eucharistic Presence in the womb of
Mary, *have mercy on us.*
Jesus, Lamb of God, in the womb of Mary, *spare us,*
O Lord.
Jesus, Holy Innocent in the womb of Mary, *graciously hear*
us, O Lord.
Jesus, Son of God and Messiah in the womb of Mary,
have mercy on us, O Lord.[13]

Litany of Loreto

Lord, have mercy on us. Christ, have mercy on us.
Lord, have mercy on us. Christ, hear us. Christ,
graciously hear us.

[13] Marta Catalano, "Litany of Jesus Christ Living in the Womb of
Mary," *All About Mary*, University of Dayton, https://udayton.
edu/imri/mary/l/litany-to-jesus-in-the-womb-of-mary.php.

God the Father of Heaven, *have mercy on us.*
God the Son, Redeemer of the world, *have mercy on us.*
God the Holy Ghost, *have mercy on us.*
Holy Trinity, one God, *have mercy on us.*
Holy Mary, *pray for us.*
Holy Mother of God, *pray for us.*
Holy Virgin of virgins, *pray for us.*
Mother of Christ, *pray for us.*
Mother of divine grace, *pray for us.*
Mother most pure, *pray for us.*
Mother most chaste, *pray for us.*
Mother inviolate, *pray for us.*
Mother undefiled, *pray for us.*
Mother most amiable, *pray for us.*
Mother most admirable, *pray for us.*
Mother of good counsel, *pray for us.*
Mother of our Creator, *pray for us.*
Mother of our Savior, *pray for us.*
Mother of the Church, *pray for us.*
Virgin most prudent, *pray for us.*
Virgin most venerable, *pray for us.*
Virgin most renowned, *pray for us.*
Virgin most powerful, *pray for us.*
Virgin most merciful, *pray for us.*
Virgin most faithful, *pray for us.*
Mirror of justice, *pray for us.*
Seat of wisdom, *pray for us.*
Cause of our joy, *pray for us.*
Spiritual vessel, *pray for us.*
Vessel of honor, *pray for us.*
Singular vessel of devotion, *pray for us.*
Mystical rose, *pray for us.*
Tower of David, *pray for us.*

Tower of ivory, *pray for us.*

House of gold, *pray for us.*

Ark of the covenant, *pray for us.*

Gate of Heaven, *pray for us.*

Morning star, *pray for us.*

Health of the sick, *pray for us.*

Refuge of sinners, *pray for us.*

Comforter of the afflicted, *pray for us.*

Help of Christians, *pray for us.*

Queen of angels, *pray for us.*

Queen of patriarchs, *pray for us.*

Queen of prophets, *pray for us.*

Queen of apostles, *pray for us.*

Queen of martyrs, *pray for us.*

Queen of confessors, *pray for us.*

Queen of virgins, *pray for us.*

Queen of all saints, *pray for us.*

Queen conceived without Original Sin, *pray for us.*

Queen assumed into Heaven, *pray for us.*

Queen of the most holy Rosary, *pray for us.*

Queen of families, *pray for us.*

Queen of peace, *pray for us.*

Lamb of God, who takest away the sins of the world,
  spare us, O Lord.

Lamb of God, who takest away the sins of the world,
  graciously hear us, O Lord.

Lamb of God, who takest away the sins of the world, *have
  mercy on us.*

Pray for us, O holy Mother of God,
  that we may be made worthy of the promises of Christ.

Let us pray: Grant, O Lord God, we beseech Thee, that we
Thy servants may rejoice in continual health of mind and

body; and through the glorious intercession of Blessed Mary ever Virgin, be freed from present sorrow and enjoy eternal gladness. Through Christ our Lord. Amen.

Litany of Penance

Lord, have mercy on us. Christ, have mercy on us.

Lord, have mercy on us. Christ, hear us. Christ,
    graciously hear us.

God the Father of Heaven, *have mercy on us.*

God the Son, Redeemer of the world, *have mercy on us.*

God the Holy Ghost, *have mercy on us.*

Holy Trinity, one God, *have mercy on us.*

Incarnate Lord, *have mercy on us.*

Lover of souls, *have mercy on us.*

Savior of sinners, *have mercy on us.*

Who didst come to seek those that were lost,
    have mercy on us.

Who didst fast for them forty days and nights,
    have mercy on us.

By Thy tenderness toward Adam when he fell,
    have mercy on us.

By Thy faithfulness to Noah in the ark, *have mercy on us.*

By Thy remembrance of Lot in the midst of sinners,
    have mercy on us.

By Thy mercy on the Israelites in the desert,
    have mercy on us.

By Thy forgiveness of David after his confession,
    have mercy on us.

By Thy patience with wicked Ahab on his humiliation,
    have mercy on us.

By Thy restoration of the penitent Manasseh,
    have mercy on us.

By Thy long suffering towards the Ninevites, when they
went in sackcloth and ashes, *have mercy on us.*

By Thy blessing on the Maccabees, who fasted before
the battle, *have mercy on us.*

By Thy choice of John to go before Thee as the preacher
of penance, *have mercy on us.*

By Thy testimony to the Publican, who hung his head
and smote his breast, *have mercy on us.*

By Thy welcome given to the returning Prodigal,
have mercy on us.

By Thy gentleness with the woman of Samaria,
have mercy on us.

By Thy condescension towards Zacchaeus, persuading
him to restitution, *have mercy on us.*

By Thy pity upon the woman taken in adultery,
have mercy on us.

By Thy love of Magdalene, who loved much,
have mercy on us.

By Thy converting look, at which Peter wept,
have mercy on us.

By Thy gracious words to the thief upon the cross,
have mercy on us.

We sinners beseech Thee, *hear us.*

That we may judge ourselves and so escape Thy
judgment, *we beseech Thee, hear us.*

That we may bring forth worthy fruits of penance,
we beseech Thee, hear us.

That sin may not reign in our mortal bodies,
we beseech Thee, hear us.

That we may work out our salvation with fear and
trembling, *we beseech Thee, hear us.*

Son of God, *we beseech Thee, hear us.*

Lamb of God, who takest away the sins of the world,
  spare us, O Lord.
Lamb of God, who takest away the sins of the world,
  graciously hear us, O Lord.
Lamb of God, who takest away the sins of the world,
  have mercy on us.
Christ, hear us. *Christ, graciously hear us.*
O Lord, hear our prayer.
  And let our cry come unto Thee.

Let us pray: Grant, we beseech Thee, O Lord, to Thy faithful, pardon and peace, that they may be cleansed from all their offenses, and also serve Thee with a quiet mind, through Christ our Lord. Amen.[14]

Litany of the Powerlessness of Jesus

A proud and self-reliant man rightly fears to undertake anything, but a humble man becomes all the braver as he realizes his own powerlessness; all the bolder as he sees his own weakness; for all his confidence is in God, who delights to reveal His almighty power in our infirmity and His mercy in our misery. (attributed to St. Francis de Sales)[15]

Through Your choosing to do nothing on Your own but
  only what You saw Your Father doing, Jesus, Lord of
  Lords, *save us.*
Through Your choice to become a tiny embryo enclosed
  in the womb of Your Mother Mary, unable even to

[14] By St. John Henry Newman.
[15] In *Bible Promises Made Easy* by Mark Water (Alresford, Hampshire: John Hunt Publishing, 2001), 35.

breathe on Your own, Jesus, Creator of the Universe,
save us.

By Your submission to the limitations of time when You
exist in eternity, Jesus, the Alpha and Omega, *save us.*

Through Your choice to become the lost sheep sought
out by the shepherds who "left the ninety-nine" on
the night of Your birth, Jesus, the Good Shepherd,
save us.

Through Your need to be nourished at Your Mother's
breast when You are "a table laden with abundance,"
Jesus, Eucharistic Feast, *save us.*

Through Your defenselessness during the flight into
Egypt, when You had to rely on Joseph's protection,
Jesus, our Deliverer, *save us.*

By the dependence of Your childhood in the home of
Mary and Joseph, when You needed their time, attention, and love, Jesus, our Provider, *save us.*

By Your obedience to Mary and Joseph, even though You
have dominion over the universe, Jesus, Ruler of All
Nations, *save us.*

Through Your refusal to turn "stones into bread" when
You were famished after forty days in the desert,
although You later multiplied the loaves for Your
hungry disciples, Jesus, Bread of Life, *save us.*

Through Your desperate request to the Father in the Garden of Gethsemane to save You from the sufferings
that You anticipated, Jesus, our Savior, *save us.*

For surrendering Yourself to the judgment of Pontius
Pilate, Jesus, our Just Judge, *save us.*

Through Your choice to be identified as a criminal and a
blasphemer, causing the high priest to tear his robe,
Jesus, our Great High Priest, *save us.*

Through Your silence, "opening not your mouth" in defense as You were accused unjustly, Jesus, the Word, *save us.*

By not resisting a crown of thorns, You who crown us with glory and honor, Jesus, King of Kings, *save us.*

Through the weakness You experienced on the way of the Cross, causing You, through whose strength we can do all things, to fall three times to the ground, Jesus, Our Stronghold, *save us.*

Through Your acceptance of Simon's help on the Way of the Cross, although You carry the whole world on Your shoulders, Jesus, Strength of Pilgrims, *save us.*

Through surrendering Yourself to the gibbet of the Cross, when You have exalted us with great power, Jesus, enthroned on the praises of Israel, *save us.*

Through Your refusal to "save yourself" as the crowds jeered at You while You hung upon the Cross, yet You still promise to "*save us* from the hands of our enemies," Jesus, Source of Eternal Salvation, *save us.*

Through Your refusal to demand justice, and through Your choice to forgive and make excuses for Your friends and enemies who crucified You, Jesus, our Justice, *save us.*

Through the deep thirst You suffered as You cried out from the Cross, although You had miraculously drawn water from a rock to quench the Israelites' thirst in the desert, Jesus, Source of Living Water, *save us.*

Through submitting Yourself to the greatest abandonment possible, that of Your true Father, yet You never leave the temple of our hearts, and You promise to be with us until the end of the age, Jesus, Son of God, *save us.*

By Your entering into our greatest moment of powerlessness, death, and allowing it, for a moment, to appear victorious, Jesus, Author of Life, *save us.*

Through Your raising of the only son of the widow of Nain, yet You let Your dead Body remain in the arms of Your widowed Mother, Jesus, the Resurrection and the Life, *save us.*

Through Your choice to remain imprisoned in tabernacles throughout the world, yet You break our chains of sin and death, Jesus, our Freedom, *save us.*

Let us pray: Jesus, our Savior and Redeemer, even though You are all powerful, You embraced our human powerlessness throughout Your life on earth, and You embrace it still in the Eucharist. You did nothing of Your own will but only of the will of Your Father. Help us, who are intrinsically powerless, to abandon our illusions of control and self-sufficiency, and give us the humility to relinquish our own wills and plans, so that like You, Jesus, we will do nothing on our own but will do only the Father's will, and may we find true freedom and perfect power by always asking Your help. Amen.[16]

Prayer before Holy Communion

Almighty and Eternal God, behold I come to the sacrament of Your only-begotten Son, our Lord Jesus Christ. As one sick, I come to the Physician of life; unclean, to the Fountain of mercy; blind, to the Light of eternal splendor; poor and needy, to the Lord of Heaven and earth. Therefore, I beg of You, through Your infinite mercy and generosity, heal my weakness, wash my

---

[16] By the Franciscan TOR Sisters.

uncleanness, give light to my blindness, enrich my poverty, and clothe my nakedness. May I thus receive the Bread of Angels, the King of kings, the Lord of lords, with such reverence and humility, contrition and devotion, purity and faith, purpose and intention, as shall aid my soul's salvation.

Grant, I beg of You, that I may receive not only the sacrament of the Body and Blood of our Lord but also its full grace and power. Give me the grace, most merciful God, to receive the Body of Your only Son, our Lord Jesus Christ, born of the Virgin Mary, in such a manner that I may deserve to be intimately united with His mystical Body and to be numbered among His members. Most loving Father, grant that I may behold for all eternity face to face Your beloved Son, whom now, on my pilgrimage, I am about to receive under the sacramental veil, who lives and reigns with You, in the unity of the Holy Spirit, God, world without end. Amen.[17]

Prayer of Entrustment to the Womb of Mary

Almighty God, Heavenly Father, who have placed me, by Baptism, in the womb of the Virgin Mary beneath her Immaculate Heart to be together with Your Son and ever more conformed to Him by the power of the Holy Spirit, grant that I may wholeheartedly embrace my dependence on You as I place all my trust in my Mother Mary.

May I never scorn my weakness which Your Son also assumed, but may I always be grateful to be little and helpless, knowing that without You, I can do nothing. Under the cloak of St. Joseph, her spouse, May I find in her a refuge against every danger, and in her womb, a hiding place invisible to the ancient foe.

---

[17] By St. Thomas Aquinas.

May I know that I am loved perfectly like Jesus by Joseph and Mary, those parents who, receiving everything from You, will always provide for all of my needs. Through the same Christ our Lord. Amen.

Radiating Christ

Dear Jesus, help me to spread Your fragrance wherever I go. Flood my soul with Your spirit and life. Penetrate and possess my whole being so utterly that my life may only be a radiance of Yours. Shine through me and be so in me that every soul I come in contact with may feel Your presence in my soul. Let them look up and see no longer me but only Jesus! Stay with me, and then I shall begin to shine as You shine, so to shine as to be a light to others. The light, O Jesus, will be all from You; none of it will be mine. It will be You, shining on others through me. Let me thus praise You the way You love best, by shining on those around me. Let me preach You without preaching, not by words but by my example, by the catching force of the sympathetic influence of what I do, the evident fullness of the love my heart bears to You. Amen.[18]

Sub Tuum Praesidium

We fly to your protection, O Holy Mother of God. Despise not our petitions in our necessities, but deliver us always from all dangers, O glorious and blessed Virgin. Amen.

---

[18] Attributed to St. John Henry Newman.

Thomistic Litany of Humility

O Jesus, meek and humble of heart, *teach me.*

From all pride and its effects, *deliver me, Jesus.*

From coveting greatness for its own sake or to excess,
    deliver me, Jesus.

From contempt of You and Your law, *deliver me, Jesus.*

From a puffed-up self-image, *deliver me, Jesus.*

From claiming to be a self-made man, *deliver me, Jesus.*

From ingratitude for Your gifts, *deliver me, Jesus.*

From thinking that I have earned Your gifts by my
    effort alone, *deliver me, Jesus.*

From boasting of having what I do not have,
    deliver me, Jesus.

From excusing my faults while judging others,
    deliver me, Jesus.

From wishing to be the sole possessor of the skills
    I have, *deliver me, Jesus.*

From setting myself before others, *deliver me, Jesus.*

From all vainglory, *deliver me, Jesus.*

From craving praise for its own sake, *deliver me, Jesus.*

From looking for flattery, *deliver me, Jesus.*

From withholding glory from You, *deliver me, Jesus.*

From showing off to the harm of my neighbor,
    deliver me, Jesus.

From presumption and false self-confidence, *deliver me, Jesus.*

From boastfulness, *deliver me, Jesus.*

From hypocrisy, *deliver me, Jesus.*

From the excessive need to be fashionable,
    deliver me, Jesus.

From obstinacy and contention, *deliver me, Jesus.*

From disobedience, *deliver me, Jesus.*

From all false humility, *deliver me, Jesus.*

From forfeiting my dignity as a child of God,
   deliver me, Jesus.
From burying the talents that You gave me,
   deliver me, Jesus.
From an unreasonable fear of failure, *deliver me, Jesus.*
From avoiding my true vocation, *deliver me, Jesus.*
From despair at my weakness, *deliver me, Jesus.*
In the ways of humility, *teach me, Jesus.*
To know my limits and my strengths, *teach me, Jesus.*
To acknowledge the depravity of my past sins,
   teach me, Jesus.
To acclaim You as the author of all the good I do,
   teach me, Jesus.
To put my confidence in You, *teach me, Jesus.*
To be subject to You and Your Church, *teach me, Jesus.*
To be subject to others for Your sake, *teach me, Jesus.*
To revere Your presence in others, *teach me, Jesus.*
To rejoice in Your gifts in others, even the gifts unseen,
   teach me, Jesus.
To do great things by Your help and for Your glory,
   strengthen me, Jesus.
To seek greatness in heavenly things and lasting virtue,
   strengthen me, Jesus.
To do my best even when unnoticed, *strengthen me, Jesus.*
To put my share of Your gifts at Your service,
   strengthen me, Jesus.
To be neither puffed up by honor nor downcast by
   shame, *strengthen me, Jesus.*
To do penance for my sins and those of others,
   strengthen me, Jesus.
Above all, to strive to love You with all my being,
   strengthen me, Jesus.

And to love my neighbor as myself, *strengthen me, Jesus.*
In Your name, I pray. Amen.[19]

Veni Sancte Spiritus

Holy Spirit, Lord of light,
from the clear celestial height
Thy pure beaming radiance give.

Come, Thou Father of the poor,
come with treasures which endure;
come, Thou light of all that live!

Thou, of all consolers best,
Thou, the soul's delighted guest,
dost refreshing peace bestow;

Thou in toil art comfort sweet;
pleasant coolness in the heat;
solace in the midst of woe.

Light immortal, light divine,
visit Thou these hearts of Thine,
and our inmost being fill:

If Thou take Thy grace away,
nothing pure in man will stay;
all his good is turned to ill.

Heal our wounds, our strength renew;
on our dryness pour Thy dew;
wash the stains of guilt away:

---

[19] Br. Joseph Martin Hagan, "A Thomistic Litany of Humility," *Dominicana*, February 20, 2017, https://www.dominicanajournal. org/a-thomistic-litany-of-humility/.

Bend the stubborn heart and will;
melt the frozen, warm the chill;
guide the steps that go astray.

Thou, on us who evermore
Thee confess and Thee adore,
with Thy sevenfold gifts descend:

Give us comfort when we die;
give us life with thee on high;
give us joys that never end. Amen.[20]

[20] Roman Missal translation.

IMAGE CREDITS

Unless otherwise specified, images are from Wikimedia Commons.

1. *Song of the Angels* by William-Adolphe Bouguereau (Forest Lawn Museum, Glendale, CA) © Alamy (BM06C9).
2. *Madonna and Sleeping Child* by Giovanni Battista Salvi da Sassoferrato (Louvre Museum, Paris, France) © incamerastock / Alamy (2JRAFCK).
3. *The Virgin and Child Embracing* by Giovanni Battista Salvi da Sassoferrato (National Gallery, London, England) © Peter Horree / Alamy (J44B8Y).
4. *Madonna and Child* by Massimo Stanzione (National Museum of Capodimonte, Naples, Italy).
5. *Rest on the Flight into Egypt* by Bartolomé Esteban Murillo (Hermitage Museum, Saint Petersburg, Russia).
6. *The Adoration of the Shepherds* by Bartolomé Esteban Murillo (Prado Museum, Madrid, Spain).
7. *Innocence* by William-Adolphe Bouguereau (private collection) © classicpaintings / Alamy (EHWTR1).
8. *Virgin of the Napkin* Bartolomé Esteban Murillo (Museum of Fine Arts, Seville, Spain).
9. *The Madonna and Child* by Anthony van Dyck (Dulwich Picture Gallery, South London, England).
10. *Madonna with Child and Angels* by Giovanni Battista Salvi da Sassoferrato (Galleria nazionale d'arte antica di palazzo Corsini, Rome, Italy).

11. *Madonna in the Meadow* by Raffaello Sanzio da Urbino (Museum of Art History, Vienna, Austria).

12. *Madonna and Child* by Simon Vouet (Musée des beaux-arts de Marseille, Marseille, France) © Peter Horree / Alamy (E9MP1D).

13. *The Virgin and Child with Flowers* by Carlo Dolci (National Gallery, London, England).

14. *Madonna and Child* by Francesco Granacci (Metropolitan Museum of Art, New York City).

15. *Madonna and Child with Saints Francis and Jerome* by Francesco Francia (Metropolitan Museum of Art, New York City).

16. *Virgin and Child* by Francesco Pesellino (Isabella Stewart Gardner Museum, Boston).

17. *Madonna and Child with Six Saints* by Francesco Pesellino (Metropolitan Museum of Art, New York City).

18. *Madonna and Child* by Pietro Perugino (Walters Art Museum, Baltimore).

19. *Virgin and Child in Glory* by Bartolomé Esteban Murillo (Walker Art Gallery, Liverpool, England).

20. *Virgin and Child with a Rosary* by Bartolomé Esteban Murillo (Prado Museum, Madrid, Spain).

21. *Virgin and Child with St. John* by Carlo Maratta (Museum of Art History, Vienna, Austria).

22. *The Nativity* by John Singleton Copley (Museum of Fine Arts, Boston).

23. *Virgin and Child with Angels* by Bartolomeo Cavarozzi (Museum of Fine Arts, Houston).

24. *Virgin and Child with Four Angels* by Gerard David (Metropolitan Museum of Art, New York City).

25. *Madonna and Child* by Anonymous.

26. *Madonna and Child* by Filippo Lippi (Uffizi Gallery, Florence, Italy).

27. *The Virgin and Child* (*The Madonna of the Book*) by Sandro Botticelli (Museo Poldi Pezzoli, Milan, Italy).

28. *Madonna and Child* by Fra Angelico (Bode Museum, Berlin, Germany).

29. *Madonna and Child with the Lamb of God* by Leonardo da Vinci (Museo Poldi Pezzoli, Milan, Italy).

30. *The Virgin of the Lilies* by William-Adolphe Bouguereau (private collection).

31. *Madonna and Child* by Giovanni Bellini (Metropolitan Museum of Art, New York City).

32. *Madonna and Child* by Domenico Ghirlandaio (National Gallery of Art, Washington, DC).

33. *The Virgin and Child Enthroned* by Ludovico Brea (Museo Poldi Pezzoli, Milan, Italy).

34. *Madonna and the Sleeping Christ Child* by Charles Alphonse du Fresnoy (Musée des Beaux-Arts d'Agen, Agen, France).

About the Author

❖

Fr. Boniface Hicks, O.S.B., is a Benedictine monk of Saint Vincent Archabbey in Latrobe, Pennsylvania. He has provided spiritual direction for many men and women, including married couples, seminarians, consecrated religious, and priests — even while completing his Ph.D. in computer science at Penn State University. He is an on-air contributor for We Are One Body Catholic Radio and has recorded thousands of radio programs on theology and the spiritual life. He has extensive experience as a retreat master for laity, consecrated religious, and priests. He is the director for Spiritual Formation at Saint Vincent Seminary and the director of the Institute for Ministry Formation. He authored the book *Through the Heart of St. Joseph* and co-authored, along with Fr. Thomas Acklin, the books *Spiritual Direction* and *Personal Prayer*.

Sophia Institute

Sophia Institute is a nonprofit institution that seeks to nurture the spiritual, moral, and cultural life of souls and to spread the gospel of Christ in conformity with the authentic teachings of the Roman Catholic Church.

Sophia Institute Press fulfills this mission by offering translations, reprints, and new publications that afford readers a rich source of the enduring wisdom of mankind.

Sophia Institute also operates the popular online resource CatholicExchange.com. *Catholic Exchange* provides world news from a Catholic perspective as well as daily devotionals and articles that will help readers to grow in holiness and live a life consistent with the teachings of the Church.

In 2013, Sophia Institute launched Sophia Institute for Teachers to renew and rebuild Catholic culture through service to Catholic education. With the goal of nurturing the spiritual, moral, and cultural life of souls, and an abiding respect for the role and work of teachers, we strive to provide materials and programs that are at once enlightening to the mind and ennobling to the heart; faithful and complete, as well as useful and practical.

Sophia Institute gratefully recognizes the Solidarity Association for preserving and encouraging the growth of our apostolate over the course of many years. Without their generous and timely support, this book would not be in your hands.

www.SophiaInstitute.com
www.CatholicExchange.com
www.SophiaInstituteforTeachers.org

Sophia Institute Press is a registered trademark of Sophia Institute.
Sophia Institute is a tax-exempt institution as defined by the
Internal Revenue Code, Section 501(c)(3). Tax ID 22-2548708.